Advance Praise for *Moviemaking in the Classroom*

"Filled with stories of student possibilities, fascinating lessons, and how to get from where you are to where you want to be, this book is a wonderful resource for any teacher wanting to create powerfully memorable learning with their students. *Moviemaking in the Classroom: Lifting Student Voices Through Digital Storytelling* is the best combination of video-as-art and video-as-communication that I've seen. The reader will learn from and be encouraged by Pack's many insights, as well as the ideas of exceptional educators whose messages enhance the activities and pedagogical exploration. Shane Frakes's 'tell me without telling me' idea is one I will bring to the schools I work with right away. Thank you, Jessica, for crafting this exceptional book."

—**Rushton Hurley**
Executive Director of NextVista.org

"Storytelling enhances learning, and Jessica Pack has created a wonderful resource to help any educator bring compelling moviemaking into their teaching practice. *Moviemaking in the Classroom* includes a background on the history, impact, and brain science of storytelling, along with an explanation of the process, including project ideas, examples linked with QR codes, input from K–12 educators, assessments, and quick-start lessons, making it a fantastic guide for digital filmmaking. It's a useful source for teachers in any content area who are interested in helping their students speak their truth and learn to communicate in this dominant medium."

—**Tim Needles**
Media and Art Educator, Author of *STEAM Power*, @timneedles

"I taught film as well as integrated media production in my self-contained classes, and it took me a DECADE to develop the skills and activities that Jessica makes oh-so-easy to acquire in *Moviemaking in the Classroom*. Like it or not, our students are ALL media students today and this book gives educators a fast, academically relevant way to add video production to their classes, from simple to sophisticated. Don't miss out on leading video-based lessons because it looks time-consuming or you have no experience. Jessica Pack makes adding video to your classroom smooth and easy."

—**Jon Corippo**
Author, *The Eduprotocol Field Guide, Book 1* and *Book 2*, and
***The EduProtocol Field Guide Math Edition*;**
Contributing Author, *100 No-Nonsense Things that ALL Teachers Should STOP Doing*; Helpful Guy

"Part manual, part memoir, part edtech cookbook, Jessica Pack's *Moviemaking in the Classroom* is a state-of-the-art guide to digital storytelling in the classroom, for both the novice and the experienced. Her inspiring journey as a teacher is joined by a host of fellow educators sharing tips, tools, successes, and best practices for making the K–12 classroom a studio where ideas are given sound and form, student voices are raised, and learning is fostered through creativity. Pack makes a compelling case for making digital storytelling the core of how students find their voices to succeed in their studies and in life."

—**Frank Guttler**
Media Literacy Coach and Founder, Lights, Camera, Learn!

"*Moviemaking in the Classroom* is an inspirational resource and guide for educators at all levels who are introducing students to the process of moviemaking and digital storytelling. Jessica Pack provides a wealth of startup strategies, curricular integrations, mini lessons, assessment tools, management tips, research and rationale. Woven throughout is her passion for providing a powerful platform for student voice through the stories they create. The success of her technique is evident in the stories and examples she shares."

—Julie Jaeger
PD Coach and Consultant, Educator of Gifted, Tech Integrationist

"Jessica Pack has given us a book that is vibrant, thoughtful, and necessary. In classrooms where students and their stories are embraced, the potential for deep connection with their learning and achievement is super-charged. Jessica shows us, through examples and practical strategies, how to use the medium of digital storytelling to empower our learners. The world our students live in today is dependent on the confident, flexible use of media to tell powerful stories to make change, solve problems, and create a better world for all of us. *Moviemaking in the Classroom* will help you teach your students to do just that—beautifully."

—Rebecca Mieliwocki
2012 National Teacher of the Year

"Digital storytelling can transform the learning experience for our students. Jessica Pack is a natural storyteller who will pull you in and get you excited about trying the lessons she outlines in her book. Through stories, rich examples, and resources, you will have a massive toolkit to bring moviemaking to life in your classroom. We know that our students all have a story to tell. This book will show you how to give your students that voice to tell theirs."

—Laurie Guyon
Coordinator for Model Schools, Washington-Saratoga-Warren-Hamilton-Essex BOCES, and NYSCATE Trainer (@smilelearning)

"In her book, Jessica Pack demystifies classroom filmmaking by addressing obstacles and presenting solutions. The provided lessons are ready to use and break down the moviemaking process into smaller, more approachable steps. This book is a great addition to the bookshelf of any K–12 teacher who wants to experience the incredible impact filmmaking can have on student learning."

—Tracy Walker, M.Ed.
Middle School Teacher, Novato Unified School District

"Jessica Pack has given educators a powerful blueprint to engage ALL students in digital storytelling. *Moviemaking in the Classroom* is a must-read for anyone who wants to provide meaningful student-driven instruction."

—Dr. Brian McDaniel
California Teacher of the Year and Global Teacher Prize Finalist

Moviemaking
in the Classroom

**Lifting Student
Voices Through
Digital Storytelling**

*Emily and ACPS,
Happy Storytelling!*

Jessica Pack

For Grades
3-12

Moviemaking in the Classroom
Lifting Student Voices through Digital Storytelling

Jessica Pack

Library of Congress Cataloging-in-Publication Data

Names: Pack, Jessica, author.

Title: Moviemaking in the classroom : lifting student voices through digital storytelling / Jessica Pack.

Description: First Edition. | Portland, OR : International Society for Technology in Education, [2021] | Includes bibliographical references and index.

Identifiers: LCCN 2021023593 (print) | LCCN 2021023594 (ebook) | ISBN 9781564849281 (Paperback) | ISBN 9781564849267 (ePub) | ISBN 9781564849274 (PDF)

Subjects: LCSH: Storytelling--Data processing. | Literature and technology. | Internet in education. | Digital storytelling. | Storytelling in education.

Classification: LCC LB1042 .P27 2021 (print) | LCC LB1042 (ebook) | DDC 371.33/44678--dc23

LC record available at https://lccn.loc.gov/2021023593

LC ebook record available at https://lccn.loc.gov/2021023594

First Edition

ISBN: 978-1-56484-928-1

Ebook version available

Printed in the United States of America

ISTE® is a registered trademark of the International Society for Technology in Education.

Director of Books and Journals:
Colin Murcray

Acquisitions Editor:
Valerie Witte

Production Editor:
Stephanie Argy

Copy Editor:
Joanna Szabo

Proofreader:
Lisa Hein

Indexer:
Kento Ikeda

Book Design and Production:
Danielle Foster

Cover Design:
Christina DeYoung

Peer Reviewers:
Kelli Duhaney, Gwynn Moore, Adrianne Rose, Pam Sprute

About ISTE

The International Society for Technology in Education (ISTE) is home to a passionate community of global educators who believe in the power of technology to transform teaching and learning, accelerate innovation and solve tough problems in education.

ISTE inspires the creation of solutions and connections that improve opportunities for all learners by delivering: practical guidance, evidence-based professional learning, virtual networks, thought-provoking events and the ISTE Standards. ISTE is also the leading publisher of books focused on technology in education. For more information or to become an ISTE member, visit **iste.org**. Subscribe to ISTE's YouTube channel and connect with ISTE on Twitter, Facebook and LinkedIn.

Related ISTE Titles

Awesome Sauce: Create Videos to Inspire Students, Engage Parents and Save You Time, by Josh Stock (2020)

Teach Boldly: Using Edtech for Social Good, by Jennifer Williams (2019)

New Realms for Writing: Inspire Student Expression with Digital Age Formats, by Michele Haiken (2019)

To see all books available from ISTE, please visit **iste.org/books**.

About the Author

Jessica Pack is a California Teacher of the Year and CUE Outstanding Educator who has been teaching middle school for 16 years. She has used digital storytelling as an instructional strategy for most of her career and regularly presents on the topic at both regional and national conferences. In addition to her role as a classroom teacher, Jessica co-hosts a podcast called *Storytelling Saves the World*, available on iTunes and SoundCloud. After spending a decade as a teacher-consultant for DIGICOM Learning, a nonprofit aimed at promoting and supporting digital storytelling in Southern California classrooms, she served as an ISTE Digital Storytelling PLN Leader. You can connect with Jessica via Instagram or Twitter @Packwoman208 and find her on the web at **jessicapack.com**.

Dedication

To every student who ever walked through my classroom door, and to those I have yet to meet—this book is for you. Your voices matter.

With gratitude to my parents, Roger and Deanna, who taught me to work hard and dream audaciously.

And for Brandon, whose love and encouragement I could not live without.

Contents

Introduction   viii

Part 1 Why Story?

Chapter 1   My Storytelling Journey   3

Chapter 2   Why Stories Resonate   11

Chapter 3   The Power of Student Voices   21

Part 2 The Nuts and Bolts of Storytelling Through Moviemaking

Chapter 4   The Storytelling & Moviemaking
             Process   35

Chapter 5   Integrating Moviemaking into the
             Curriculum   55

Chapter 6   Storytelling Mini Lessons   75

Chapter 7   Removing Barriers from Storytelling   89

Part 3   **Getting Started with Students**

Chapter 8   Quick-Start Moviemaking
Lesson Ideas   105

Chapter 9   Storytelling in Online Learning
Environments   123

Acknowledgments   131

References   133

Index   136

Introduction

Fourteen years ago, I started on my storytelling journey when one of my students discovered iMovie, prompting me to consider how student-created filmmaking could be leveraged for academic benefit. As a classroom teacher, it was difficult to find many resources for moviemaking in core content areas. In the beginning, I searched diligently for lessons or strategies that could apply to my educational setting. Many guides were geared only toward media specialists and most books treated the topic of moviemaking as a prospective pit stop on a technological highway of possibilities. The purpose of this book is not only to showcase the power of digital storytelling, but also to provide classroom teachers and instructional coaches with concrete suggestions pertaining to how and why we should integrate moviemaking into our curriculum.

Moviemaking in the Classroom: Lifting Student Voices Through Digital Storytelling is divided into three parts. In the first section, readers will learn about my journey as a storytelling teacher. They will also come to understand the role stories have played in our history, the brain science behind storytelling, and how it impacts our learning. Find out what makes stories effective and how student-created movies can redefine what learning looks like in classrooms and communities.

The second part of this book will outline the nuts and bolts of the moviemaking process. After reading, educators will be able to purposefully plan lessons with moviemaking in mind. One of my goals for this book is to help teachers develop multiple opportunities for students to create digital stories within a single academic year. So, this section covers effective lesson design, pathways for integration, audiovisual mini lessons, and assessment. It also identifies potential barriers to the storytelling process and how to remove them.

The third and final part of this book outlines five quick-start lesson ideas teachers can immediately use in their classrooms, as well as best practices for storytelling in online environments. All of these lessons include templates and rubrics that allow teachers to create opportunities for storytelling right away. If you'd like to jump right to this section to suit your immediate needs, please do! However, I do hope you'll want to explore the rationale and process discussion in the first two sections at some point. As leadership expert Simon Sinek teaches, starting with the *why* makes the whole picture clearer.

As you read, I hope you can feel my passion for digital storytelling through moviemaking. Whether you are just embarking on your journey or are a seasoned storyteller, my hope is that this book will both inspire and empower you as you move forward. Room 208 kids have told some incredible stories over the years, and I know your students will, too.

Part 1

Why Story?

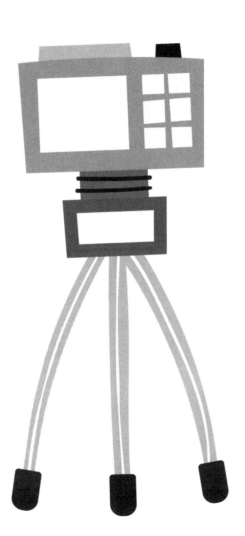

Chapter 1

My Storytelling Journey

One of the best moments of my professional life involved standing on the beach at the Salton Sea, the smell of sulfur filling my nostrils and the crunch of fish scales under my feet. Once a resort for the Hollywood crowd during the glamorous Golden Age of film, the Salton Sea is a deep, man-made lake that rests 236 feet below sea level. It is known locally as a place where the salt content is so high that many marine species can't survive. Thousands of dead fish litter the sandy shoreline and though their bodies decompose, their scales remain. Agricultural runoff has polluted the waters, causing a sulfuric smell that travels for miles during the summer months—I can some-times smell it from my classroom door at the other end of the Coachella Valley. Still, standing there in triple-digit heat on a Saturday in September, I couldn't have been happier as I listened to the director give his actors a pep talk.

"What we need to remember is that these characters are on a quest. They could literally save this kid's entire future if they find the buried treasure." The director, Jebari, sat on a picnic table and leaned forward to rest his elbows on his knees. He spoke earnestly as the actors listened carefully.

"This kid's family is falling apart. He's desperate and it's our job to help viewers understand that. Maybe somebody who watches our movie will have parents going through a divorce, too. This story works because it's relatable. We've spent a lot of time preparing. Now, let's get out there and make it happen. Oh, and Isaiah? Spit out your gum, man."

There was a flurry of sand as the crew scrambled to turn on iPads, sweep up boom mics, and grab extra copies of the script. The actors double-checked their costumes and the producer yelled for places. Someone found the clapper board. Jebari put on the headphones that were connected to the microphone. He took a deep breath.

"Quiet on the set, guys. And . . . action!"

Watching my middle school students carry out the complex enterprise of shooting off campus was a wonder to behold. Aside from occasionally troubleshooting technical issues or giving advice on how to adapt to the numerous lighting challenges created by the hot desert sun and the sparkling blue water, I wasn't involved much. They ran the show. It was my job simply to supervise and enjoy the backdrop of the sea as it glittered in nearly every shot.

Months later, as my students walked on stage to accept an award for their movie, entitled *Lost Ships*, I was so proud that I cried. That spring, Jebari walked the red carpet at the Palm Springs International Film Festival because he earned a student director's pass to attend panel discussions on filmmaking. All because of a little digital story that started out in my classroom and proved what I had always known: Storytelling opens doors.

As a teacher, my discovery of storytelling happened quite by accident. I certainly didn't start out filming on location, or filming at all, actually. During my second year of teaching, my principal asked for volunteers to pilot our district's first technology initiative: a 24/7 MacBook program. There were only two of us who were willing to take part in the pilot. In retrospect, as a new teacher, I was living in a perpetual state of flexibility, constantly being forced to think on my feet as I learned how to teach middle schoolers. It was probably this adaptability that allowed me to approach the 24/7 program without fear and to embrace instruction in a digital environment.

A few weeks into the pilot, I remember watching my students create digital plot diagrams when a hand tentatively raised into the air. The hand belonged to one of my favorite students—even though teachers are not supposed to have favorites. Kasen was a bright kid, with a mile-wide mischievous streak and the kind of sarcastic wit typical of middle school boys.

"Um, excuse me, Mrs. Pack . . ." he said. "I found something really cool. Actually, a lot cool. I accidentally clicked on something. Did you know we can make movies on our computers? No, seriously. There's this star icon . . ."

Inadvertently, Kasen had discovered iMovie, and that was the moment my instructional paradigm shifted. Even now, fifteen years later, I can picture it clearly in my mind: The afternoon sun filtering through the skylight in my classroom, 35 students craning their necks to peer curiously over at Kasen's desk. There was an undercurrent of excitement and whispered voices asking where to look for the star icon. We didn't learn any more about plot diagrams that day. Instead, we went on one of the most important sidebars of my career, an exploration that would shape not only my professional practice, but my teaching philosophy, too. It would also function as the catalyst in my quest to understand what it means to be a storyteller, and ultimately discover my own voice as a teacher-filmmaker.

Educational Context

There is a high level of need in my community and many students, families, and teachers face educational challenges. My school district serves approximately 21,000 students, 29% of whom are English language learners. At my school, 84% of the families we serve live below the poverty line, and the vast majority of students are Hispanic and from Spanish-speaking homes. Only 39% of our high school graduates are categorized as "prepared for college" according to Policy Analysis for California Education (2018), and the reality is that most of our students will not attend a four-year university. In fact, many of our students rarely venture outside of the Coachella Valley even as adults, despite being only about 90 miles away from Los Angeles.

Being a part of a technology pilot program appealed to me because it meant putting other options on the table for my students. Letting them know that they had more choices at their disposal—if they worked hard to acquire digital age skills—could change the trajectory of their lives. Kasen's discovery of iMovie made a brand-new pathway available: content creation. What could students create if given the opportunity? What effect could this have on their education? On their future? Ideas began to percolate, and I started to think this all-important question: *What if?*

Becoming Storytellers

The first movies my students ever made were tied directly to core content standards, and we made them shortly after Kasen's discovery. Students were given a standard and asked to find a way to teach viewers about the concept being covered. One of my students, Isabel, created a wonderful movie about density and buoyancy. In one scene, she took a beach ball into her pool and demonstrated that it could float, unlike other objects which only dropped to the bottom. I remember watching her video after school with my team teacher, Julie. We were absolutely floored that it was possible for kids to be in their home environment, demonstrating academic understanding, and investing time and effort outside of the classroom in a way we had never seen before. The videos were not technical marvels. In fact, they were fairly low resolution because students used the iSight cameras on their laptops to film everything. The concept of better film equipment had not even entered our minds yet. However, this was our first inkling that making movies could be an expression of content mastery.

Next, my students created public service announcements about any problem they could identify in our community. Kasen's project was about the danger of talking to strangers. He refused to write a script and decided to wing the process instead, casting his father as the stranger and his little brother as the hapless victim. Not knowing much about the production process yet, I let him blaze his own trail and simply hoped for the best. Kasen told me that he cradled his MacBook in his arms as he filmed his dad walking up the pathway to the front door. The footage ended up taking on a point-of-view quality, almost like something out of *The Blair Witch Project*. The entire plot consisted of the stranger knocking on the door, having a friendly chat with a child, and then asking to use the phone. Once the stranger was allowed inside, he grabbed the student. The door drifted closed, the screen faded to black, and bright red letters appeared: "Don't Talk to Strangers. Or Else."

I remember trying to convince Kasen that he should refilm to get rid of the shaky footage. I remember suggesting that perhaps he would like to add some music or a title slide. My intention was to convince him to make a slightly more polished product, but he held firm and insisted that his PSA was the perfect embodiment of his vision, shaky camera and all. As I look back on it now, I realize that Kasen was right. He held on to creative control instinctively, and I—as almost all teachers do at one time or another—thought I needed to assert my role as the instructor. However, no matter how much I wanted to polish it up to be closer to my view of perfection, I couldn't ignore the insistent feeling that there was something truly special about Kasen's project. Fortunately, the arrival of a visitor helped me understand just what was so extraordinary.

Piloting the 24/7 MacBook program meant that my classroom often received guests. Everyone in and out of the district seemed to want to see firsthand what it was like to teach in a digital environment. One of the technology leaders for my district, Dr. Lee Grafton, stopped by unexpectedly one day, bringing a community member in tow. She introduced the guest as David, who lived in Palm Springs and was interested in helping the district in some way. I assumed that meant he was a potential donor for program expansion, so I talked at length about the types of work my students were able to accomplish using computers. When I mentioned that we had recently discovered how to make movies, his eyes lit up. "Show me," he said.

I played Isabel's movie on buoyancy and raved enthusiastically about how it demonstrated her mastery in science. David was polite, but seemed slightly detached, maybe even disappointed somehow. I couldn't read him very well, so I was surprised when he asked, "Do you have anything else?"

I can't explain why I showed him Kasen's PSA, but I did. Ten seconds into the movie, David's expression grew intense. He edged in front of me, got down on his knees next to the desk, and proceeded to watch the video three more times. After the fourth viewing, he looked up at me from the Macbook on the desk and said, "Now, that's a story."

They left shortly thereafter, with none of the effusive comments I was used to hearing. I wasn't sure what to make of the visit, until Dr. Grafton called me after school that day.

"Thank you for letting us visit. David was very impressed. He's thinking and he wants to help, he's just figuring out how."

"That's nice," I responded. "I'm glad he liked seeing the kids' work. Who is he, again? A local resident?"

She laughed. "His name is David Vogel. He just retired and moved to the desert full-time. He's looking for a way to give back. Oh, and he's the former president of Walt Disney's Buena Vista Motion Pictures Group."

As a result of David's classroom visits that year, he founded a nonprofit called DIGICOM Learning, whose mission was to promote and support digital storytelling in Southern California classrooms. At the time, I was the only teacher he had met who was integrating moviemaking into core content areas. So, after about a year, David brought me on board to teach colleagues about how and why they should implement moviemaking in their classrooms. By then, I had plunged headfirst into the idea that making movies to assess student understanding was far more effective and

engaging than any multiple-choice test I could write. I applied the writing process to scripting and taught my students how to draw storyboards. With a background in photography as a hobbyist, I had a good eye for shots, so I started systematically teaching kids about film angles. At this point, my learning focus was wrapped up in the technical aspects of moviemaking, but over time I grew to understand that it is the story that really matters.

I ended up working as a teacher-consultant for DIGICOM Learning for the next decade. Throughout my tenure at DIGICOM, I had the opportunity to work with hundreds of teachers across Southern California classrooms. My conversations with David and the other film industry professionals who worked there honed my under-standing of what it means to tell a story digitally. Sure, my technical knowledge increased in terms of composition, editing techniques, and capturing quality sound. However, the true value of my association with David and the people at DIGICOM was realizing that the heartbeat of a movie is the story it tells. You can use fancy editing tricks and film beautiful footage in HD, but if there is no emotional appeal, no conflict to resolve, no triumph of the human spirit, then you don't have a story. What you end up with is a nice multimedia piece that isn't nearly as memorable.

Moviemaking has had a transformative effect on my classroom. Over time, it has become an integral part of the social fabric among students, a defining charac-teristic of what it means to be a room 208 kid. Evidence of that can be seen on our classroom YouTube channel, which has established a powerful legacy. When kids arrive for a new academic year, they already seem to know what to expect, espe-cially those with older siblings or cousins who were previously in my classes. Many of them discover the channel and watch most of its contents over the summer before I even meet them. It is not unusual for a student to ask on the first day, "When do we make our first movie project?"

Helping students craft stories and discover their voices has been incredibly gratify-ing. Through mentoring them, I have become a storyteller, too, creating content that is important to me in both my personal and professional life. Now each year, part of the magic of room 208 is a mutual respect for and recognition of the importance of our lived experiences. My students know that the very best stories come from their own lives, and they are the ones in charge. This type of agency is a mighty force in the learning process.

Storytelling Advocacy

The longer you teach, the more opportunities you have to observe the pendulum swing. It seems as if schools and districts all over the United States are constantly adopting new programs and strategies, hoping to close the achievement gap and improve standardized test scores. Some of the programs aren't even really new; they are simply repackaged to suit another wave of implementation. As a veteran teacher, you become used to this pendulum swing and begin to expect that everything has a shelf life. So, it is rather remarkable that digital storytelling has been an unshakable pillar of my instruction for such a long time.

I continue to integrate moviemaking because I have seen how potent learning can be when there is an audience outside of the immediate classroom. The idea that others will view one's work lends authenticity to the learning experience. Some of my most quiet and shy students have blossomed into confident creators, amplifying their voices beyond what anyone thought was possible. Educators are always looking for ways to engage disinterested students, and moviemaking has proven alluring even for the most resistant learners. I have never met a kid who did not have something to say. I have never met a kid who didn't want to make a movie. Passionate ownership is the natural result of student choice and voice. This is why I've spent more than a decade advocating for moviemaking in core subject areas.

In my classes, we constantly circle back to the notion that everyone has a platform. Everyone has the potential to raise their voice to make an impact. Students need to be taught how to appropriately leverage their platform to further the ideas and issues that are important to them. Preparing kids to learn, create, and share in this vast digital environment is essential to life in the digital age. Storytelling has the power to shape and change the world. Let's equip our kids to be storytellers.

Chapter 2
Why Stories Resonate

Students today are the YouTube and TikTok generation. They are eager to broadcast their ideas. They want to know that they are seen, heard, and valued. To a certain extent, that has always been true. However, now more than ever, it is essential for us to teach our students how to communicate in such a way that their voices will be heard amid the sea of other voices every-where in media and on the internet. There is an art to storytelling, an ebb and flow of thoughts that create an emotional current. This current is what compels viewers to pay attention to what someone has to say. Explicitly teaching students how to express their thoughts in words and images is a powerful, transferable skill.

Social media is the perfect example of modern storytelling. When you scroll through Facebook or Instagram, what content makes you stop? People create and publish videos every day and evidence is right there in our feeds. Amid this vast ocean of available content, an important question is whether or not our students possess the skills they need to effectively communicate worthwhile messages. Anyone can make a video with the latest dance trend, but fewer people can generate truly compelling subject matter that educates or inspires. There is a distinct, multimodal skill set that contributes to successful digital com-munication, the most important element of which is developing the story itself.

A History of Storytelling

As humans, we are predisposed to respond to stories. Evidence of storytelling dates back to prehistoric times, as seen in the paintings inside the Chauvet Cave in southeastern France. Created during the Upper Paleolithic era, the paintings are estimated to be around 32,000 years old (Groeneveld, 2017). Historians have speculated that the images on the walls are both concrete and representational, indicating our early ancestors had imagination. The most wonderful conclusion that can be drawn from the existence of this prehistoric art is the idea that we have always been wired to tell stories, to listen and learn from them.

It makes sense that archaeologists found multiple hearths inside the Chauvet Cave, too, not just because charcoal was an artistic medium, but also because campfires are the setting for oral traditions. Stories have been retold from one generation to another around the world—origin stories, cautionary tales, and cultural teachings. For hundreds of thousands of years, stories had to be remembered and repeated without the benefit of writing. Which begs the question, did ancient people just have really excellent memory capacity? Or was there something deeper at play?

Written language developed in Mesopotamia and Egypt around 3000 BCE. The oldest known written story is the *Epic of Gilgamesh*, which was carved onto a series of tablets. This epic poem was about a Sumerian king and his heroic adventures. Gilgamesh was handsome, athletic, and two-thirds divine. He displayed the gamut of human emotions and engaged in all sorts of behavior that caused a myriad of conflicts involving both the people he ruled and the gods who attempted to keep him in check. Emotional themes pertaining to relationships, the nature of leadership, and overcoming obstacles made this story important in the ancient world—so important that ancient Sumerians even carved the story on tablets and buried them beneath city walls (Andrews, 2015). It continues to resonate today, retold in short stories and graphic novel format, often still included in humanities textbooks at many grade levels. The lasting appeal of Gilgamesh speaks to a strong story's ability to endure.

Various story genres emerged over time, such as Greek myths around 1000 BCE and Aesop's fables in the 500s BCE. The invention of paper, woodblock printing, and the printing press all occurred during the common era, making stories more portable and able to be distributed farther distances. Modern storytelling became more visual, first with the advent of photography in 1826 and then the development of motion photography in 1878. Motion photography used multiple cameras to capture still images in quick succession, which were then combined to create a motion picture. *The Horse in Motion* (Muybridge, 1878) is often cited as the foundation for the motion picture industry. Film production companies formed in the early 1900s and,

Norman McKee, SIXTH-GRADE TEACHER

"In African culture, there is a line of griot, who have innate talent to be storytellers. The griot skills are passed on biologically and culturally through marriage, but they are also cultivated. Traditionally, in the African community, if one recognizes that a child has the ability to become a griot, then others will teach him. Oral tradition is directly connected to the griot, so griots must know the history of our people.

In the modern African American community, storytelling is not necessarily groomed the same way as it is in the African community. However, individuals can recognize storytellers when they see them—whether they know it or not. I grew up in an area where there were people with griot in their blood and I would be around them quite a bit. The stories they told were not always cultural; they were street stories delivered through conversation. As a child, I was able to sit by them and listen as they crafted their skills and their stories.

Today, storytelling helps students place value on education. Why do we as educators tell children about how education will be important in their future? We need to show them right now because they don't have that foresight. When learning is connected to a product—in this case, a story—that synthesizes all of their skills, all of their modalities, then they see importance."

during the silent era, live music often accompanied screenings. New cinematic tech-niques emerged as sound, special effects, and color developed. Even as movies were widely distributed, broadcast radio and the premiere of network television brought stories into homes. Radios and televisions became the modern equivalent of prehis-toric campfires.

The idea of mass appeal and access, combined with the invention of the personal computer, is what eventually opened the door for the development of digital story-telling. Digital storytelling is the process of creating and sharing stories using digital tools. Multimedia incorporates words, images, and sounds, all of which are used to tell digital stories. This modality of storytelling is impactful because it can be produced by anyone with access to digital tools and shared via many different web platforms. It is pervasive in every aspect of our culture, from advertising to blogs, video games, social media, and virtual reality. There is an immediacy to our capacity for telling digital stories and no shortage of ways in which we can share our thoughts and ideas. Understanding the far-reaching history of storytelling helps us better appreciate the digital tools at our fingertips, and the possibilities therein. BBC documentarian Daniel Meadows describes digital stories as "multimedia sonnets from the people" (Coomes, 2011) I love his definition, not just because it sounds soulful and romantic, but because it strikes upon the individualized nature of the stories we tell.

With constantly evolving tools and increasing ways for everyday people to create and share, the digital age is the most exciting time for storytelling yet. So, what makes stories resonate? Why do they continue to be a centerpiece of our culture? Two things: emotion and brain science.

What Makes Stories Effective?

Storytelling has nothing to do with the medium used. Whether you are a writer, photographer, podcaster, artist, or moviemaker, the most important component of your work is the story you choose to tell. In this way, storytelling is program-agnostic. Whether your students are making a movie using an app or drawing a comic on paper, they are telling a story—and as Clint Eastwood says, "Story is king" (American Film Institute, 2009).

Story is the exploration of change, of what happens when a conflict occurs to alter the world in which characters live, forcing them to grow or discover new truth. Such stories ignite emotion in both the person telling the story and the person receiving it. These stories capture and hold our attention because they are compelling. At the first spark of conflict, storytellers have engaged us in the plot. They *keep* us invested by increasing tension through a series of events or challenges that must be faced. Tension builds emotional resonance because it transports us into the character's world. Once there, we are able to make inferences as well as intuitive connections between story elements. This emotional arc is so effective that many people refer to it as universal story structure.

Researchers have observed that stories light up the areas of the brain responsible for making predictions. We place ourselves in the character's shoes and then connect on an emotional plane. Plato famously explained the impact of story, saying, "Come then, and let us pass a leisure hour in storytelling, and our story shall be the education of our heroes." What he meant was those who listen to stories learn from them. They are inspired to become better, understand more, and ultimately become the heroic protagonists of their own lives (Gallo, 2017). In the education setting, this idea manifests as students write, retell, listen, and create stories. As they do, learning becomes deeply personalized.

The Brain Science of Storytelling

There is quite a bit of research published on the impact storytelling has on the brain. Educators can leverage this impact to make learning a more dynamic process. Stories stimulate specific areas in the mind that can change how we perceive and process information. The limbic system is one of the brain networks most heavily influenced by story. This system is responsible for all behavioral responses, and when it is activated by the emotional tension in stories, it can inspire people to take action

(Zak, 2014). Emotional tension is also what causes viewers or listeners to internalize the characters' experiences long after the story has ended. Therefore, emotion gives storytelling considerable staying power.

Both of the brain's language processing centers are actuated by stories. Not coincidentally, these portions of the brain are also stimulated when we are actually experiencing an event, so they give us the ability to live vicariously through the power of a strong story. There is evidence that when storytellers use sensory details, the sensory cortex engages. For example, brain scans reveal that when we hear a story that includes details about a particular scent, the part of the brain responsible for olfactory processing is stimulated (Paul, 2012). Thus, viewing or listening to a story engages many different brain networks, contributing to the strength of our experience.

Storytelling spurs the production of particular brain chemicals, too. Three main chemicals are activated in the brain by storytelling: cortisol, dopamine, and oxytocin. Cortisol is associated with formulating memories. When we hear a story, cortisol helps us remember what we've learned, making that learning "sticky" (Peterson, 2017). Important ideas are therefore more easily acquired and transferred to long-term memory. Another chemical, dopamine, regulates emotional responses and correlates with our level of engagement. It works in conjunction with oxytocin, which is the chemical that allows us to feel empathy, connect with others, and maintain good relationships. Oxytocin is also reliably activated by character-driven stories (Zak, 2014). What important information for all educators to leverage! If we want to ensure that our classrooms foster engaged students who genuinely care about content, it makes sense to utilize instructional strategies that appeal to the brain on a chemical level.

Storytelling and Learning

Human beings are innately social creatures. Stories let us transfer information and values within and across generations and cultures. They also enable us to make meaning as we relate stories to our prior experiences. The power of story is that it shapes and expands our understanding of the world through new perspectives.

Ferrés and Masanet (2017) explain that the brain's perceptual and emotional systems work together to drive cognition. They point out that the most effective educational communication strategies address the different interests that motivate students, creating emotional investment rather than apathy. Digital storytelling exemplifies such a strategy, leaving room for a variety of uses while lending itself to all grade levels and content areas.

Often, people say that reason and emotion are separate. This idea is attributed to the seventeenth-century thinker, mathematician, and scientist, René Descartes. Modern neuroscientist Antonio Damasio, the author of *Descartes' Error*, asserts that there is no distinction between reason and emotion because they are inseparable in a way that reflects our human complexity (2005). The idea that reason and emotion are tangled together explains why some concepts stick in our minds better than others. When we rely heavily on instructional strategies based on information delivery, we are appealing only to reason. Students' emotions are not engaged, so the learning is more easily forgotten. The reality is stories and memory function together (Brown et al., 2014). Narrative provides both meaning and a mental framework for assimilating future information and experiences with existing schema. This does not mean that digital storytelling is only applicable to narrative writing; rather, the challenge is to identify and elaborate the story of whatever content is being covered in the classroom.

The net effect of leveraging storytelling in education can be observed in the amount of ownership students feel over the products they create. As Daniel Pink explains in his book, *Drive*, people crave autonomy, mastery, and purpose (2013). These three factors can serve to motivate even the most reluctant individuals. Over the years, some of the very best movies my students have produced have been created by those who were most challenged by the traditional academic environment. They found the self-driven nature of storytelling appealing. The fact that there is never just one right answer, that the finished product depends on decisions executed by the creator, is attractive to students. They have an innate desire to demonstrate mastery because it feels good to know one is doing well. Students are not only motivated when the work is authentic to them as individuals, but also when the creative purpose of a movie project is greater than just the classroom audience. For this reason,

David Vogel, FOUNDER OF DIGICOM LEARNING, FORMER PRESIDENT OF WALT DISNEY'S BUENA VISTA MOTION PICTURES GROUP

"Story is the single most important element of a movie. The first thing we want is to capture attention. Then we want to hold attention. Finally, we want the person whose attention we have borrowed to walk away with something meaningful. The more meaningful it is, the better the story is in terms of its value to the listener—and the more that person will have had a satisfying experience. When a story works, it's evident. You can feel it, and it sticks in your mind.

My observation about the dilemma of public education, the way it's been constructed, has to do with the push for the standardization of children. The truth is that children are absolutely individual human beings, and though they may be young, they all have voices. The most important thing we can do is provide opportunities for them to use their voices, whether about their lives or their schoolwork. All human beings want to express themselves. So do children, within the context of what educators are offering them. The combination of images and words is singularly important in society today. Giving kids a chance to say something—and the freedom in which to say it—is wildly engaging."

establishing authentic audiences plays a key role in the storytelling process. All stories are created with an audience in mind. For my students, the audience for whom they most routinely create are their peers and our community at large. YouTube and social media provide immediate access to these viewers, while other audiences—such as film festivals, city officials, or community activism groups—require more purposeful outreach in order to connect.

Much of the learning process in the digital age is dependent on the use of technology. In a study conducted in Palm Springs Unified School District in Palm Springs, California, researchers from University of California Riverside found that students who engaged in digital storytelling had a significantly higher sense of self-efficacy pertaining to

technology than students who did not. Vu, Warschauer, and Yim (2019) theorize that this could be attributed to the level of engagement students experience while telling digital stories. Investment in the learning process translates into increased student effort. As students locate and strategically utilize the tools needed to bring their stories to life, they come to believe passionately in their own ability to succeed.

The Endgame

Educators want to see their classroom communities thrive. We want to design effective instruction that reaches all students. Though there are many different strategies that could be included in one's instructional design, the aspects of storytelling combine to create a robust opportunity for learning. Researchers have found that a student's neural network is best activated when teachers combine collaborative tasks, dialogue, classroom synergy among students, the use of technology, and multimedia communication (Ferrés and Masanet, 2017). All of these factors are amplified in digital storytelling as students use technology and employ multimedia to communicate through moviemaking.

Attentive brains, sticky learning, genuine engagement, intrinsic motivation—these are the natural byproducts of including storytelling in the curriculum. Student-created stories can be powerful artifacts of learning. My students and I have gravitated toward moviemaking as our preferred way to tell stories, and it has fundamentally changed our classroom culture. In the next chapter, you will see the incredible impact of student voices sharing stories of inclusion, empathy, and change.

Chapter 3

The Power of Student Voices

Though we are naturally drawn to stories, we are not automatically equipped to produce work that is compelling. Learning to craft messages that resonate is more than simply combining images and audio components—it is also knowing how to engage the hearts and minds of viewers so they can enhance their understanding or discover truth. Compelling stories open up viewers to new information, changing the way they perceive others and building empathy.

My students have many opportunities to create digital stories throughout the year. The goal is always to provide as many storytelling chances as possible. This allows students to build storytelling fluency, which not only results in greater efficiency in the production process but also a sense of self-efficacy. Creative confidence is what enables children to find and develop their voices.

Student voices are powerful because they are authentic. Over the years, I have found that young people are far more willing to be vulnerable or say difficult things than most of the adults I know. Digital storytelling can be an equalizer, amplifying voices that are underrepresented and providing opportunities that might otherwise be inaccessible. Storytelling can provide a social-emotional outlet by offering an avenue to process the complexities of life or share burdens of the spirit. Perhaps most importantly, storytelling can be used to expose injustice, raise awareness, and instigate change.

Storytelling as an Equalizer

Representation matters, but the sad reality is that many students do not see themselves reflected in the world around them. Ethnic identity is not valued in every quarter of society, and too often the stories of people of color are overlooked. Black and brown students have historically received the terrible message that their lived experiences are not important. Furthermore, for students who live in poverty, the lack of social and economic currency can seriously impact their self-esteem. I have worked with many children over the years who initially doubted whether they had anything worthwhile to say. They were certain that the important stories belonged to other kids, the ones who lived in nicer neighborhoods and led lives cushioned by privilege.

Digital storytelling teaches all students that they have voices, and those voices can be amplified. Further, encouraging storytelling by marginalized groups, especially about culturally relevant topics, builds a sense of pride and belonging. For example, one of my Native American students, Gina, wanted to memorialize her grandfather. He had recently passed away and was the tribal chairman of the Agua Caliente Band of Cahuilla Indians. Gina created a beautiful tribute to her grandfather's legacy, sharing both his love for his family and the ways in which he had served his people.

Because an essential component of digital storytelling is the soundtrack used to help set the mood or tone, Gina spent days looking for the perfect music. She simply

wasn't happy with anything she found, and I remember watching her sit at our class-room iMac, gazing at the screen with her hands folded in her lap. When I asked if she needed anything, Gina quietly told me that none of the music was right because it wasn't authentic—she wanted to record an original track using GarageBand to capture the sounds of her Native culture. So, I met Gina and her dad early one morning at school. He played a native instrument and sang traditional songs beautifully as Gina recorded. I will never forget the look on her face as she was finally able to complete her project. That year, her tribute to her grandfather was played at our local film festival as well as at several tribal events. Each time it was screened reinforced Gina's understanding that her voice and her culture were valued.

One of my students was incredibly passionate about Black history. Throughout the year, we studied the civil rights movement, learned about social justice leaders, and read novels and short stories from authors of color. He loved all of it, engaging in class discussion more frequently than any other student. Then, on January 31, he sent me an email inquiring about Black History Month, wanting to know what special projects I had planned for the month of February. Initially, I was thrown off balance. My instructional philosophy is that Black history should be woven into the curriculum throughout the whole year, not just relegated to one month. Didn't he see how much we had already covered? Didn't he have confidence that we would continue to expand our learning? And then I realized that his email wasn't about what we'd learned so far or what we might do throughout the rest of the year. As a Black student, he wanted to use the specific opportunity Black History Month provided to amplify his voice and the voices of other Black Americans.

The next day, as we worked at the small group table, I asked my student what type of movie project he would like to create in honor of Black History Month. After a few moments of thinking he said, "I think it would be great if we could look at achievements of Black Americans. We've done a lot of cool stuff and accomplished great things. Plus, I'm reading a biography about Frederick Douglass and I want to share what I'm learning."

The next day, we started research projects based on *The Undefeated 44* (**bit.ly/Undefeated44Site**), an online publication detailing the contributions of 44 Black Americans from a variety of industries. Students wrote poems to give context about society during each person's lifetime, while framing their major accomplishments. These poems became the narration for individual movie projects; students utilized primary source images and stock footage to bring their work to life using WeVideo. The student who sparked this project ended up having his movie screened at the local film festival, and he smiled from ear to ear as he accepted his award. Being recognized in one's community sends a powerful message of respect, acceptance, and celebration.

Middle school is a particularly difficult phase in a student's academic journey, made all the more challenging due to the emergence of cliques and the pervasive feeling that one is not understood. Creating digital stories builds empathy and connection. One of my students wanted to challenge conventional beauty standards by creating a digital story about what it is like to be a Filipino girl in today's world. She recounted a time during school picture day when several girls made fun of her appearance. My student put her heart on display, sharing her inner monologue as she looked in a bathroom mirror. Her movie depicted a journey toward self-love. At one point in the movie, when she says that she is more than just a number on a scale, she rips a picture of a blonde Barbie doll face in half. When we watched this student's movie in class, a few of the girls cried as the paper ripped. The tears on their brown cheeks showed they could relate on a deep level, and afterward the dynamics of our class shifted. My student's voice helped others realize their worth and the worth of those around them. The girls were kinder to one another, giving compliments and positive affirmations more frequently for the rest of the year.

Often, students assume they know one another based on appearances. That was true in the case of Nayef, one of the seventh-grade students in my leadership class. Because he had brown skin, other students assumed he was Mexican, but Nayef is Syrian. When the opportunity arose to tell a digital story about something personal, he opted to create a project based on his

**WATCH NAYEF'S
MOVIE, *FAMILY***

summer visit to see his family in Syria. Nayef wrote the story of his travels to an active war zone, including what it was like to jet ski on crystal blue waters one morning and then listen to missiles cruise overhead while at dinner that night. Leveraging family photos, footage from Al Jazeera, and the reenactment of certain key scenes, Nayef's story was impactful. It not only taught other students about his culture, but also shed light on what it was like to travel inside a war-torn country, and then return home to wonder about the safety of the family members left behind.

After we viewed Nayef's work in class, everyone was silent. They had no prior frame of reference for war, and few had any idea that Nayef's family spoke Arabic, not Spanish. When a few moments passed, students started asking questions. *Why did the electricity go out at one point in the story? What nearby town was destroyed by the missile? Is your family okay now?* The questions flowed, as did Nayef's answers, and our classroom community knit a little closer than it had before.

Storytelling as a Social Emotional Outlet

As teachers, our understanding of students' lives can often be limited to our in-class interactions. Sometimes, there is just so much to accomplish in one day that it can be tempting to take an all-business approach to class time. What research has shown us, however, is that it is just as important for educators to pay attention to students' social emotional states as it is to worry about content. Our students have complex inner lives, complicated home lives, and feelings that directly reflect their stability or lack of it. Divorce, illness, death, miscarriage, sexuality—all of these are issues that our students face. How can we help them process these situations? How can we support them in their learning despite whatever is going on outside of school?

Digital storytelling teaches students to process the tragedies and complexities of life. It gives them the opportunity to reframe their struggles and reclaim what hurts them. One of my students, Marina, used storytelling as a healing experience.

I noticed that she was acting differently in class one day, lethargic and disengaged compared to her normal vivacity. When we talked after class, she revealed that her baby cousin, Gio, had drowned in her grandmother's swimming pool over the weekend. The baby had been pulled from the water, resuscitated, and then taken to intensive care in an ambulance. The family was initially hopeful, but soon became devastated because Gio's brain functioning never resumed. He passed away a few days later.

WATCH MARINA'S MOVIE,
REMEMBERING GIO

I held Marina while she cried and called home to ask someone to pick her up from school. After encouraging both Marina and her parents to allow her to stay home as long as needed, I told her to let me know if she needed anything, even if it was just to talk. About a month after the funeral, Marina stood quietly by my desk one afternoon.

"It happens a lot," she said. "Toddlers drown in pools each year. I want to do something about it. I want to make a movie to tell Gio's story and I want it on YouTube. I want everyone to see, so it doesn't happen to them."

"Okay," I replied. "I can help you do that, but I think you should talk to your family first. Make sure they would be okay with you telling this story."

Marina's family was supportive, so she started the scripting process. This was not part of a class project, just something she wanted to accomplish on her own because she had already experienced the power of moviemaking and how messages can travel to broad audiences beyond the classroom walls. Marina spent hours after school writing and storyboarding. She filmed some reenactment scenes inside her grandmother's home, but the swimming pool was a sticking point. She wanted to be interviewed on camera talking about her cousin, and she wanted to do it sitting beside a pool. Just not *that* pool.

Marina asked to use the swimming pool at my house. I told her to pick a couple of students from our class that she would feel comfortable working with, so they could be her crew. I talked with her parents, filled out the field trip paperwork, and we filmed on a weekday afternoon. Many takes were required, as Marina broke down several times,

but each time we asked her if she wanted to stop, she shook her head and kept going. Clearly, telling this story was important to her and nothing was going to stand in her way—not even grief. The students who had agreed to help her were empathetic and patient through the process. They became incredibly invested in the project and shed tears of their own as they listened to Marina tell her family's story.

Marina had created many digital stories in my classroom. Her experiences in making so many different projects taught her that moviemaking was a way to educate others, so the call to action at the end of her movie was a plea to families to fence their pools. Marina called this project *Remembering Gio*. We uploaded it to our classroom YouTube channel, and she entered it in the local film festival, where it was screened and awarded a $1,000 charitable gift. The donation was made to the American Red Cross in Gio's name and Marina accepted on behalf of her entire family.

Many of my students have used storytelling as a way to come to terms with difficult situations and daunting truths. One of my students, Aubrie, made a movie called *Without Him*. The story was about her parents' separation and what it is like to live daily life without her dad, who resides in Colorado. Her next project, *One Day at a Time*, profiled her grandfather and his battle with cancer. In both instances, the power of Aubrie's voice shone, connecting

WATCH AUBRIE'S
MOVIE, *WITHOUT HIM*

others to her work and helping them to identify with her experiences. Digital storytelling builds bridges, and as we watched her stories in class, students responded.

>   *My parents are divorced, too.*

>   *I miss my mom like how you miss your dad. We're kind of the same.*

>   *My grandma had breast cancer, and now she's a survivor. It was scary watching her go through that.*

That is what classroom empathy sounds like. That is the impact of telling meaningful stories.

Julie Barda, SEVENTH-GRADE TEACHER

"I've taught using moviemaking for quite some time. Lots of different students stand out in my mind and one of the overarching connections I can make between many of them is that they were initially very shy. Even after making digital storytelling projects, I don't think they would necessarily define themselves as storytellers, but they *do* have stories to tell. Giving kids an opportunity to take their writing—which might normally just go to the teacher, get graded, and then filed away—giving them a chance to actually share their messages with the world really helps build self-confidence. For students I have had several years in a row, having multiple chances to share has fostered their sense of story and style. It has also made them more self-aware because the stories they're telling are so personal. Some of the messages they write about are the things they most need to hear, so storytelling keeps those ideas at the forefront."

Another one of my students decided to use digital storytelling as a way to talk about sexuality. She wanted to show other middle school members of the LGBTQ+ community that they are not alone. My student wrote a spoken word piece called *Butterflies* then recited it to a cool beat. She paid a lot of attention to the concept of agreement by carefully matching the video clips with her spoken audio track. She also taught herself how to animate using an iPhone app, then layered animations over some of her video clips. The result was incredible and struck a chord in our community. Not only was her work screened at our local film festival, but also at the annual Harvey Milk Diversity Breakfast in Palm Springs. This important occasion is an LGBTQ+ event that is held every year and is attended by Gay-Straight Alliances from all over the Coachella Valley. Receiving awards wasn't what was important to her, however. She garnered genuine joy out of sharing herself with others and helping others feel comfortable in their own skin, too.

Storytelling to Create Change

Just as students recognize that the world around them does not always reflect who they are and what they look like, students also know when they don't like or appreciate how they *are* portrayed. Storytelling presents a way to flip undesirable narratives so that they more accurately reflect lived experiences. Many of my students come from undocumented families, or families that include undocumented members. We live just over one hundred miles from the U.S.-Mexico border, and its proximity shapes our community. I have overheard countless comments from students over the years regarding who has papers and who doesn't, as well as whispered fears about Immigration and Customs Enforcement.

Samantha was my first-ever student who wanted to tackle a political issue in a movie project. She was reeling after the 2016 election and wanted a way to voice her concerns, to fight back against the narrative she saw on network television. Samantha chose to make a digital story about her first-generation immigrant parents. She framed her script as a letter to the newly elected president and collected footage from the news to intersperse with original clips she shot using her cell phone

Norman McKee, SIXTH-GRADE TEACHER

"I've seen some amazing results from children sharing their stories. Storytelling gives us deeper insight. Sitting in a classroom does not necessarily provide a student with the opportunity to express who they are or display all of the talents they have in their arsenal. When we tell stories, things get personal. One student of mine reached deep inside herself, contemplated a story, artistically designed it, and then put it together. She was a quiet child who didn't speak much—the kind of student I like to call an iceberg, because she didn't show a lot outwardly, but she had a lot going on below the surface. Giving her the chance to craft a digital story allowed us to forge a stronger connection."

at home. Narrating her feelings and experiences, Samantha built an argument for how immigrants contribute to society as they seek better lives for themselves and their children. The movie she created was beautiful, and as she worked at her computer in the classroom, other kids would wander over to sit next to her for a few minutes to watch as she edited. Some of them wanted to see her creative choices, but others wanted to talk about the story she was crafting.

WATCH SAMANTHA'S MOVIE, *DEAR MR. PRESIDENT*

They came from immigrant families, too. For them, it was a watershed moment to realize that kids were allowed to talk about weighty issues. The idea that serious stories could belong to anyone, not just adults, was empowering. It gave them creative permission for future stories.

A talented folkloric dancer, Samantha's ties to her community were strong and her project was widely shared. Of course, she created with our classroom YouTube audience in mind because it was important to her that her message could be broadcast with the click of a button. Samantha is graduating high school this year and she has become a local activist, working within her school and community to change perceptions about Latinx people. She has also occasionally volunteered for the campaign of one of our Hispanic state representatives, Dr. Raul Ruiz. Samantha's discovery of her voice has shaped her life since middle school. When voices are amplified, possibilities are endless.

LISTEN TO SEASON 1, EPISODE 5: "FAMILY STORIES" FROM *STORYTELLING SAVES THE WORLD.*

One of my more recent students, Niki, also wanted to raise her voice regarding the topic of immigration. In her movie *Limits*, she wondered what would happen if the world was still a single continent. Would borders still exist? A second-generation immigrant, Niki explored this intriguing question as she wrote about her family's journey. I am fortunate to host a podcast on digital storytelling with my colleague, Georgia Terlaje. Our podcast is aptly titled *Storytelling Saves the World*, and Niki was one of our guests during the first season. When asked why she felt her movie was important, she said:

WATCH NIKI'S MOVIE, *LIMITS*

"We have this amazing platform where we can make videos and share them out in the world. I feel like this was a great opportunity for me to speak out for those who don't have the courage [or] don't feel safe speaking out for themselves."

At its core, digital storytelling is about making connections between people on a human level. Both Samantha and Niki illustrate how students who are dedicated to a particular issue can change opinions and reframe existing narratives to build empathy and understanding. This happens on a viewer-by-viewer level, one heart and mind at a time. For those who might share a similar outlook, their stories offer hope and reassurance that others understand. Projects such as these let us know that

Lynn Yada, FOURTH-GRADE HYBRID ACADEMY TEACHER

"When I teach science, I try to focus on it as a way of connecting with the community. Two years ago, my students learned about the dangers of plastic straws. They used multiple sources to research how straws affect marine life, then made a presentation to give other classes at our school. When we returned to our classroom after presenting, I asked them how we could reach more people with our message. Students decided to create movies in the form of public service announcements. They also wrote letters to the Palm Springs City Council. One of the councilmembers wrote back and invited my class to meet with the city's sustainability committee, which set up a press release and used local media to distribute the PSAs students made. As a result, my class began to meet with local businesses to raise awareness about the environmental impact of plastic straws.

Since creating their PSAs, my students have continued to work within the community. Currently, the Palm Springs City Council is drafting an ordinance banning the use of plastic straws, and my students continue to advocate for environmental responsibility by helping to shape this local public policy. It's been two years, and they still occasionally appear before the council to share their learning with our community. Storytelling helped them become change agents."

we are not alone, and sometimes one voice can represent many. For those whose outlook differs, their stories offer an entry point into a larger conversation, as well as a bridge that allows viewers to glimpse the faces of the individuals behind the issues.

A Powerful Medium

Digital storytelling through moviemaking really does have the ability to build up communities, inspire action, and highlight shared struggles. Each of the personal movie projects discussed in this chapter were born out of students' extensive experiences with storytelling. The thread of storytelling is woven throughout everything we do in room 208, and these repeated exposures contribute to the development of creative confidence. Their bravery exists because they were given multiple opportunities to find their voices and learn how to amplify them. When children choose to share the messages that are important to them, they begin to change the world.

EXPLORE JESSICA'S CLASSROOM YOUTUBE CHANNEL

So, how do we help students find their voices? How do we plan standards-based lessons that include moviemaking and structure them for efficiency? How do we foster student self-efficacy? Part two will answer all of these questions and more.

Part 2

The Nuts and Bolts of Storytelling Through Moviemaking

Chapter 4

The Storytelling & Moviemaking Process

Moviemaking is essentially the writing process in action, which is why I intentionally teach students the art of storytelling. Explicit instruction is needed pertaining to story arc, how to harness emotional current, and mechanisms that can be used to build tension. Helping students develop the skills to identify and create *compelling* stories requires process repetition, as well as opportunities to dissect strong stories in order to figure out what makes them resonate.

Teachers must help students discover the story of their learning. There is a difference between digital stories and digital reports. The difference has to do with how students share the information they have learned. Are they simply reciting a list of facts, or recounting the steps of an experiment or algorithm?

Valcine Brown, **HIGH SCHOOL ENGLISH TEACHER**

"Storytelling is an opportunity for me to impart my students with a voice. Finding a way that I can help them develop their voices in authentic ways means they are empowered. I've seen passion in students that just doesn't exist when they are simply asked to write an essay. My students have done everything, from working in small groups to create 15-second digital stories to adapting and retelling entire scenes from *A Christmas Carol*. In fact, the amount of thought they invested to bring Charles Dickens's work to life showed that they completely under-stood the moral value of the story and that they could translate it into a modern-day format. The enthusiasm students displayed was incredible! They were on task and turned in quality material. It was phenomenal."

If so, then the students are creating a multimedia project that is essentially a substi-tute for a PowerPoint presentation. However, if students are able to develop a point of view from which a narrative can be told, identify a conflict, and generate emo-tional tension that culminates in a moment of triumph or revelation—then, they have crafted a story.

For English teachers, the concept of storytelling comes naturally as an extension of content they already teach. Indeed, for many of the humanities, it makes sense to integrate moviemaking wherever writing would normally occur. In history classes, students often write historical narratives based on major events, significant figures, or people in their communities. These narratives might even have a point of view challenge built in, with directions such as "retell the events of the Battle of Marathon, either from the point of view of a Persian invader or a Greek soldier." Since these types of assignments already exist in some capacity, it isn't a stretch to translate them into opportunities to tell digital stories.

Though relatively easy to integrate into the humanities, storytelling can initially be more mystifying to implement for teachers of math and science. Often, the solution in STEM areas is to isolate problems or challenges, and then identify perspectives from which they can be examined. The story of a keystone species within an eco-system, struggling to survive, perhaps written from the animal's point-of-view, is more emotionally impactful than a factual report. During one of my digital storytelling professional development classes, an AP Biology and Environmental Sciences teacher in my district actually developed this project for her students. She reported that her students were more engaged by moviemaking than they were for any other project that year.

For both the creator and the consumer, storytelling makes learning more memorable. Though there are many ways to tell digital stories, moviemaking connects with students on a level they find relatable because their natural habitats online often include video sharing. The storytelling through moviemaking process consists of several steps: Brainstorming and prewriting, scripting, visual and audio planning, feedback, asset collection, editing, revision, and publishing. The story is primarily crafted during the brainstorming, prewriting, and scripting process. The audiovisual components of a movie help determine *how* a story comes to life, establishing the mood or tone. Obtaining feedback infuses individual projects with collaboration

Sherry DiBari, SIXTH-GRADE TEACHER

"When planning lessons in math, I use extremely visual concepts as an entry point for moviemaking. I think about what I want students to see and then work backward to plan the scaffolds to help students get there. For example, in math there is the idea that fractions are based on the size of the whole, so comparing 1/4 to 1/2 isn't valid unless you have an understanding of how large the whole is and whether both of those fractions are referring to the same whole. This can be tough for students to grasp, so generating a way for students to storify this content is powerful. Anchoring their stories in the real world makes learning relevant and helps students break down other representational concepts when they encounter them."

to prevent students from creating in isolation. All of these steps pave the way for students to collect audiovisual assets, such as images, video clips, and sound files. Editing and revision are somewhat fluid activities, as students move back and forth between these stages throughout the rest of the creation process. Finally, as movies are shared with a broad authentic audience, student work is validated.

The rest of this chapter will deconstruct each of the stages of the moviemaking process. As classroom teachers, we value effective and efficient instruction. My goal is that this chapter will provide you will a clear picture of what moviemaking looks like when it is structured for student success.

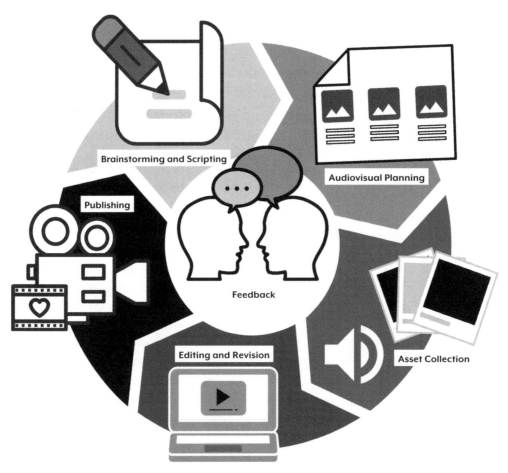

FIGURE 4.1 The Storytelling Process

Brainstorming

The brainstorming process must begin with understanding what makes a compelling digital story. Frayer models are a strategic way to help students explore this concept (see figure 4.2). Our first step is to define the word "compelling" in the center of the graphic. As a class, we watch a two- or three-minute student movie and subsequently dissect what makes it compelling. As we discuss, we formulate a list of characteristics that qualitatively express why the movie we watched was effective in its storytelling. We also consider what the student filmmaker could have done that would have been *in*effective. Teachers should act as facilitators during this exercise, and not dispensers of knowledge. Guiding the conversation and allowing students to do the work of generating ideas is critical. Remember, we are all wired for stories. Students will be able to identify much of what we want them to come up with—we just have to give them the opportunity to think and discuss in order to arrive at the conclusions needed.

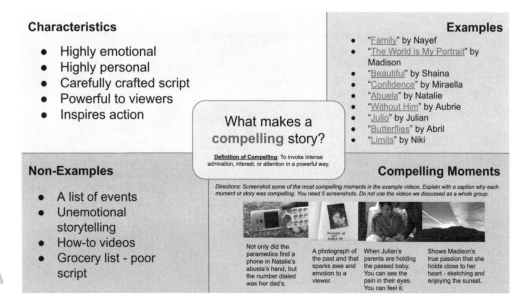

FIGURE 4.2 A sample completed Frayer model containing information about what makes a compelling story. Credit: Niki Aguilar, student

I prepopulate the third quadrant of the Frayer model with links to compelling student-made movies, and students click on whichever anchor projects appeal to them most. While watching, students pause to take screenshots of captivating moments, then embed these screenshots in the fourth quadrant of their Frayer model and explain what makes each so wholly engaging and important. In this way, students are able to spend time close viewing quality storytelling from the peers who have come before them. It also allows students to think about *why* those stories worked so well.

DOWNLOAD THE FRAYER MODEL

Following this lesson, students brainstorm their own work—in terms of both content and story arc. In the case of a personal story about one's life or struggles, story arc planning is emphasized. If a student is writing a subject matter story, however, it's important to identify the type of information that should be included in the script. For example, if writing a historical piece, which details relevant to the time period should be featured? I generally ask students to brainstorm using a circle map (see figure 4.3). This stage can be either individual or collaborative.

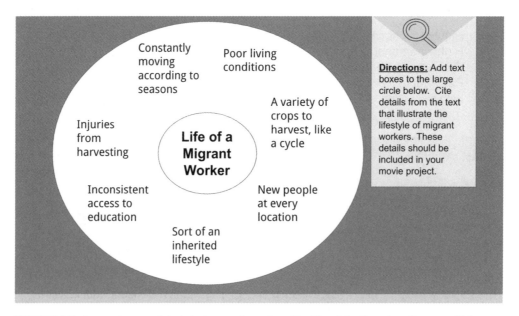

FIGURE 4.3 A sample completed circle map based on *The Circuit* by Francisco Jimenez. This circle map depicts relevant historical information to be included in a student's script.

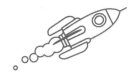

Students also need to determine which point of view they should develop in order to tell their story. Again, personal stories are easy to prewrite. It is more challenging to determine the possible points of view for other types of stories. Objects or concepts can often make strong speakers or narrators. For example, a story could be told from the point of view of a rational number, a piece of pottery from the Qin dynasty in ancient China, or a concept such as gene therapy. Some of the very best stories I have watched students create have been told from unconventional perspectives. One student told a story about prehistoric hunter-gatherer culture from the point of view of fire. The intention of the project was to relay various adaptations of early humans and how such modifications contributed to their survival. This was effectively accomplished as fire described the types of activities it observed at the heart of a hunter-gatherer encampment. Another example is from a chemistry teacher who attended one of my professional development workshops. He wrote a love story between sodium and chlorine, which culminated with these two elements becoming the compound sodium chloride, or table salt. His intention was to explore periodic elements, and the script included details about atomic number, density, and oxidation states. After the workshop, the finished product was used as an exemplar for a project the teacher then assigned to his students.

Scripting

Most stories can be divided into three segments, which screenwriters refer to as the three acts. In elementary grades, we tend to oversimplify this idea by explaining that all stories have a beginning, middle, and end. In storytelling circles, there is often a lot of pushback against these terms because they do not really connect to the function of the three acts and can lead to formulaic stories that are little more than a recitation of events in chronological order. In my classes, I refer to that type of writing as a "grocery list." If a script sounds like a list of events, the same way one might list things to buy at the store, then it's not a story yet. We know that stories center around conflicts, create tension by activating emotions, and then resolve in some sort of revelatory moment. Those qualities do not result from a play-by-play retelling.

David Vogel, one of my mentors and the retired president of Walt Disney's Buena Vista Motion Pictures Group, whom I mentioned in chapter 1, helped me understand the story arc by thinking in terms of emotional beats. In the first act, which might be considered the beginning, a character's way of life is established. Then, something new and surprising happens, causing conflict to arise. Tension increases in act two, as the character encounters difficulties and perhaps antagonists in the form of other characters, nature, or society as a whole. Finally, act three builds to a climactic moment of overcoming, which leads to some type of resolution. David used to refer to this as the "triumph of the human spirit" moment. He also helped me realize that resolution does not always mean a cut-and-dry solution. Sometimes, it means achieving a realization, heading off in a new direction, asking new questions, or leaving the ending open to interpretation. This is the explanation I give my students as I teach them about scripting. I still sometimes use the words "beginning, middle, and end" to help students conceptualize initially, but I am always careful to stress emotional beats over traditional labels (see table 4.1).

TABLE 4.1 The Story Arc

Beginning (Act 1)	The Inciting Incident What's the problem or challenge? What on-the-surface information must be shared?
Middle (Act 2)	Building Emotional Tension What events occur to build tension? What deeper information must be shared?
End (Act 3)	Triumph of the Human Spirit What moment of revelation or resolution is achieved? What information is shared that looks toward the future?

In order to aid in the script writing process, particularly as students are just starting out, using a story spine can be very helpful (see table 4.2). They are especially effective for students who require scaffolding, such as English learners or students with special needs. I first learned about the story spine from the storytelling unit of *Pixar in a Box* by Khan Academy (**bit.ly/2KikqFE**). Story spines help students conceptualize the various emotional beats required in order to tell a compelling story. Whether or

not students choose to utilize the exact words of the story spine, the structure it provides will help them build a strong script scene by scene.

TABLE 4.2 Story Spine

Story Spine	Purpose
Once upon a time there was _____.	This line provides information about the setting and the character.
Every day, _____.	Everyday life is depicted in order to set up a potential contrast once the conflict is introduced.
Until one day, _____.	An inciting incident occurs, and conflict is created! Something happens or changes to alter the state of everyday life.
Because of that, _____.	The character works toward achieving a goal, executing a plan, or seeking a solution.
Because of that, _____.	More complications arise, even as subplots resolve or minor goals are achieved.
Until finally, _____.	The revelation of truth, the achievement of a goal, or the moment of triumph occurs.
And ever since that day _____.	The action is wrapped up, a lesson is learned, and life takes on new meaning.

I have also developed other story templates to utilize with my students. Many different kinds of poems work incredibly well with any content area. At one point or another, nearly every teacher has asked their students to write some type of "getting to know you" poem at the beginning of the year. The BioPoem and the very similar "I Am" poem offer ideal support for scripting about a variety of concepts. These poem structures can be effectively used to write about people, places, or thematic ideas. They can be written from any point of view and the lines of the template can be rearranged as needed to fit the emotional beats of the story arc. (An "I Am" poem lesson plan is included in part 3 of this book.)

I also like to use well-known poems as anchor texts and help students script their movies using the original works as inspiration. One of my favorite

Virginia Gamboa, HIGH SCHOOL
ENGLISH TEACHER

"Students need to plan. Most of storytelling is about the process, not the product. The process of writing everything down, knowing what their shots are going to look like, what sentences they are going to narrate using a voiceover—all of those decisions need to be made from the outset. Once students have the words down, the visuals will come easily. If a student has had to go back into a text to find evidence to help them craft a narrative, they are better prepared to transition into the process of actually creating the movie itself. So, I never let students start to film or edit without some kind of concrete plan."

beginning-of-the-year projects is based on the poem "Where I'm From" by George Ella Lyon. It is an excellent example of the storytelling arc and, because students are experts on themselves, it serves as a good entry point to delve into the storytelling process. A second iteration of the project can then be accomplished with content, such as writing from the point of view of a character or a significant historical figure.

Other writing templates I've developed have been suited to specific lessons and the types of information I wanted to elicit from students. The key with any template is to allow students to maintain creative control. Moving lines around, choosing when to follow word patterns or when to change them, adding or subtracting lines—all of these creative choices should remain in the students' hands. The point of a template is to provide a suggestion; make sure students know that up front. Making movies is deeply personal, even when the content is standards-based. It is important to honor individual student choices because it sets the tone for the kinds of open-ended projects that we eventually want students to undertake.

Audiovisual Planning

Close to 60% of any moviemaking cycle should be spent on preproduction. Once a script is written, it is tempting to think that adequate plans have been made. However, both the visual and audio components must be determined before students even think of filming or editing. Predictably, some students are reluctant to engage in this process. They are so caught up in their ideas, they have a false sense of self-confidence that can lead them to impulsively carry out the production phase. This often results in errors during filming. On large-scale productions, these mistakes can generate a need to reshoot certain footage which often simply isn't possible. Another common impulse is to rush through planning in order to get to the excitement of the shoot, but that is also a grave mistake—one I frequently committed early in my moviemaking journey with students. The lesson to be learned: *Good* projects are able to come together during the production process to make a somewhat effective message. *Great* projects are the result of careful consideration and deliberate preparation.

My students use two formats for audiovisual planning: story-boards (see figure 4.4) and two-column notes (see table 4.3). Whichever type of planning students choose to leverage, it is a nonnegotiable step in the moviemaking process. The main benefit is they spend less time browsing aimlessly when seeking audio-visual assets because they know exactly what they are looking for from the outset. Storyboarding forces students to identify

DOWNLOAD THE STO-RYBOARD TEMPLATE

the images needed in order to tell a particular story. Creating a storyboard helps students see how much can be communicated in the visual aspect of their movie. Sometimes scripts can be trimmed because of the amount of information that comes across visually. The sounds required to tell a story effectively should also be identified ahead of time. Audio components to note on the storyboard include dialogue, narration, music, and voiceovers. A few guiding questions when it comes to planning sound are:

1. Which parts of the script will be narration as opposed to dialogue exchanged by characters?

2. What type of music will be used to establish mood?

3. What type of sound effects are needed to make a story more immersive for the viewer?

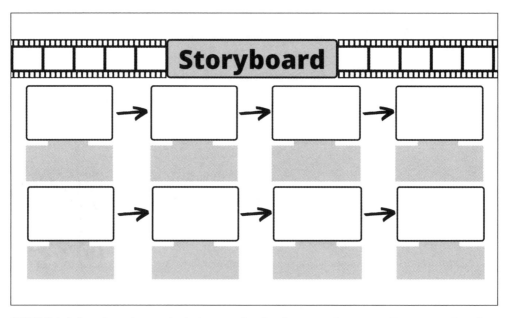

FIGURE 4.4 Storyboards must include space for sketches as well as notes. Notes typically reflect film angles, dialogue, or other pertinent information.

One of the drawbacks to storyboarding is that students with limited artistic skills can sometimes be reluctant to engage. No matter how many times I reassure students that their drawing skills are not being evaluated, some need a different planning strategy in order to feel comfortable. In those situations, I introduce two-column notes (see table 4.3). Students create what is essentially a T-Chart, with one column labeled "visual" and the other column labeled "audio." In the picture column, students jot notes about their desired visuals. This information can range from specific film angles for situations that involve video recording, to descriptions of preferred images that students plan to search for using copyright-free sources. In the audio column, students essentially copy their scripts. Once voiceovers and dialogue are listed, it is easy to see whether the visuals match.

TABLE 4.3 Sample Two-Column Notes

IRRIGATION HAIKU POEM	
Visual	**Audio**
Video clip of running water in river or stream. (Stock footage.)	Voiceover: Rivers are the key. (Running water sound effect.)
Video clip of water running through canal, or screenshot of an irrigation system diagram. (Either stock footage or screenshot of the irrigation system I drew.)	Voiceover: Water flows through gates to fields. (Running water sound effect cont.)
Video clip of grain running through someone's hands into a basket. (Stock footage or copyright-free photo.)	Voiceover: Stable food supply. (No sound effects.)

Lynn Yada, FOURTH-GRADE ONLINE TEACHER

"For a lot of my students, storytelling helps with their self-esteem. Those who may not excel at traditional academics tend to excel in moviemaking. The storyboarding process in particular is very accessible to them. Being able to draw to clarify your ideas is powerful, especially for a struggling student."

Feedback

Meaningful, timely feedback regarding student work is essential. Opportunities for feedback need to occur at regular intervals throughout the scripting and planning process. As a secondary teacher, I typically serve around 120 students per year since I teach block classes comprising language arts and social studies. Some of my single-subject colleagues see upwards of 180 students per day, so giving personalized feedback can present a legitimate logistical challenge.

One strategy is to utilize pitch groups, which take a writer's workshop approach to story concepts and scripting. Typically, an in-class pitch group consists of no more than four or five students. These students listen to one another's story ideas and drafts, while also providing feedback on visual and audio planning components. The groups function as a first line of defense against stories that don't work. Through conversation, it soon becomes obvious if a story is confusing, incomplete, or missing emotional resonance. Rather than just being an avenue for pointing out areas that need improvement, pitch groups also reinforce what students are doing well. Peer validation is valuable, and hearing the creative choices others are making can often help shy storytellers create more boldly.

In order for pitch groups to run effectively, the process of giving and receiving feedback has to be modeled. To do this, I often personally undertake the assignment I am asking my students to produce (or, a similar assignment if seeing my work would influence student work too greatly). As a whole class, we read my script. Then, I ask for feedback. At first, students are not quite certain that they are actually supposed to critique my work. It doesn't take them long to engage, however, because how often have they been asked to provide feedback *to a teacher* instead of just receiving it?! I ask students to focus solely on story at first. What works? What doesn't? Which emotions are activated? Is there a section that reads too much like a grocery list? Who is my audience—can you tell? When a student offers a vague piece of feedback, I tell them I am confused and need more, which prompts them to elaborate. This is how you build the concept of being critical friends, as opposed to giving and receiving critical cop-outs. If a group struggles to see the distinction, I find that table 4.4 helps clarify what is needed. It is also important for students to see adults respond to criticism productively. If they see me accepting critical feedback with gratitude and using that feedback to ponder aloud my options for improvement, then a culture of growth begins to develop.

TABLE 4.4 Critical Cop-Outs vs. Critical Friends

Critical Cop-Outs	Critical Friends
Your video looks great!	I like how you used the bird's-eye view to help communicate that your character felt small and helpless in the face of danger.
You did a good job.	You have a good concept for your video, but I think you need to reshoot some of your scenes. There was some backlighting and a few distractions.
Your video wasn't very good.	I am unsure about the concept of your video. I'm not sure what point you were trying to communicate. I think rewriting the script would help and a reshoot might be needed.

For projects with greater complexity, pitch groups might meet several times throughout the planning and production process. Sometimes they will meet to review storyboards or two-column notes and provide recommendations for improvement. Most often, I ask pitch groups to meet a second time in order to review a first draft of the movie project once it is roughly edited. Group rosters are preserved because students have already built an element of trust having shared their stories from the scripting stage. Whenever groups meet, specific goals are articulated from the outset. Goals might center around the content of the story, or they might center around audio/visual aspects of moviemaking. A shared Google Doc is used to record feedback. (See figure 4.5 for sample student feedback. Use the QR code on this page to access and download a blank form.) It is gratifying to listen to student conversations during second or third meetings, because students will often recall advice that was given during prior sessions and comment on how suggestions were utilized.

DOWNLOAD A COLLECTION OF SCALE FEEDBACK FORMS

SCALE Feedback Form

S	**STORY -** • The story was interesting and different from most stories I have heard. • There were 3 acts, your intro, your process, and your aftermath. • It was detailed and made sense.
C	**CAMERA -** • There were only a couple things that were filmed and they were just a bit shaky. • There were a lot of images from the internet. Maybe include more of yourself by using images from your life?
A	**AUDIO -** • I couldn't always hear your voice. It was loud and then quiet. • The music was a bit overpowering. • The music sparks emotion; I liked how it changed throughout different parts of your movie.
L	**LOOK -** • There wasn't any backlighting in the clips that were filmed. Good job! • I would have liked more video clips though. Remember, sometimes video communicates more than just photos.
E	**EDITING -** • The images weren't still. They had movement. • There wasn't much agreement. You would say a couple different lines but the image would stay the same. • The end slide was unique and I liked the font you used!

FIGURE 4.5 Student feedback from a Google Doc. Credit: Niki Aguilar

As a result of overhearing student conversations during pitch groups, I can easily identify the students in each class who are most in need of teacher feedback. Students who require more support to get their stories on track can benefit from individual script conferences or sometimes just a few well-placed comments in their Google Doc. Leaving voice feedback is another effective strategy; I like to use the Google Chrome Mote extension for this purpose. When it is important for an entire class to receive teacher feedback before progressing, then do not be afraid to shelve a project for a few days in order to give yourself the requisite time. Subpar student movies are generally not a product of poor editing. Usually, poor products result

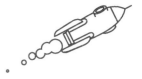

from imperfect scripts. So, if there is any point at which feedback is most essential, it is before production progresses further.

On occasions when projects are time sensitive, pitch groups can be boiled down to partner review. The same types of feedback goals are established for partners as for groups. However, the major change is that the quantity (and sometimes quality) of feedback that students receive can be lacking. Part of the beauty of feedback comes in hearing diverse opinions about one's work. For this reason, I highly recommend that teachers set aside time for at least one pitch group session.

In any feedback situation, it is important for students to have a common lexicon they can draw upon during discussion. How to develop this transferrable vocabulary is covered in chapter 6.

Asset Collection

Once students have finished planning, they are ready to collect the video clips, still images, and audio files needed for their movie. The vast majority of the time, my students leverage whatever materials are available to them via copyright-free sources first. My school district happens to have a paid subscription to WeVideo, so students utilize the media library included in the program; it consists of both video clips and images. Adobe Spark also features some free images for students to choose from, and nearly all browser-based editing programs have the ability to import images or video clips from Google Drive, social media, or the web. To streamline production, help students identify appropriate free to use and share media sources, such as Pixabay, Videvo, Pexels, and SoundBible. Teach them how to conduct advanced searches for images that are free to use and share, then show them how to locate citation information as needed.

When students are unable to find the necessary images or videos, they might choose to film original footage. Likewise, if a project is intended as an opportunity to shoot outside of the classroom, then students need to be taught how to record in landscape mode on their mobile devices. They also should have some knowl-edge of camera angles, how to frame a shot, and how to ensure that cameras remain steady.

As students collect assets, it is a good idea to teach them how to organize. Many of my students find it relatively easy to create a folder in their Google Drive accounts, then save all of their resources there, while other students prefer to create a media folder inside of their WeVideo accounts. I try not to dictate which method is best, allowing students the chance to choose their workflow whenever possible. The concept I emphasize is that being disorganized will slow their production process, so it is better to have a specific approach to asset collection.

Editing and Revision

Movies truly come together in the editing phase, not just in terms of compiling all of the media to create a whole, but also in terms of conceptual quality. Editing teaches students to persevere through challenges as they problem-solve how to bring their stories to life. Typically, I do not spend much time teaching students how to use edit-ing programs. Rather, I show them where the in-app media is located, how to import files, and then turn them loose. Inevitably, kids are able to figure out how to use the programs without any type of extensive teacher-led lesson. As questions arise, I offer guidance on an individual, "just in time" basis, then enfranchise those students to teach others as needed. Eventually, student experts emerge, and my job becomes mostly about circulating the room to simply enjoy watching students create.

Occasionally, certain features of editing programs will need to be explicitly taught. I usually choose to do so in small groups with students who are ready. These fea-tures might include the use of multiple tracks to produce animation effects, color retouching, or the use of green screen. It doesn't make instructional sense to require everyone to sit through a tutorial on how to use advanced editing features unless it is directly relevant to their current project.

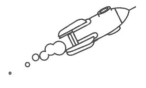

Publishing

When students create for authentic audiences, something magical happens. Not only do they invest more time, energy, and effort in their movie, but they also develop a deeper sense of ownership. Creating a movie project is profoundly personal, no matter what content is being covered. Students gain pride from work they have poured themselves into, and they become eager to share. As Rushton Hurley, a well-known advocate for digital storytelling, says, "When students know others will see their work, they want it to be *good*. When it's just for the teacher, they want it to be *good enough*" (2017). I know this statement is true because I have seen it proven time and again over the years.

There is no audience as powerful as peers. That concept is what makes social media venues like TikTok and YouTube so appealing. Young people will eagerly listen to one another's advice and perspectives—consider the number of gaming and makeup tutorials, unboxing videos, and vlogs that are popular among students. Having a classroom YouTube channel taps into that online culture and creates a space where voices can be amplified.

Even if teachers choose not to leverage video sharing platforms, there are still many ways to ensure that students create for authentic audiences. One powerful avenue is the student film festival. My district has hosted a regional student film festival, in conjunction with the nonprofit DIGICOM Learning, for more than a decade. It has provided a place for student- and teacher-created stories to be valued and celebrated as they are screened. The Palm Springs community has been incredibly supportive, with city officials, local business owners, and a variety of organizations often present. A film festival is a wonderful opportunity for students' families to see and honor the work of their children; it sends the message that student voices are both respected and appreciated. Several others student film festivals have developed in the Coachella Valley, and some schools and neighboring districts have even begun to host their own festivals. It should be noted that such celebrations are not

Georgia Terlaje, ELEMENTARY INSTRUCTIONAL COACH, FIFTH-GRADE TEACHER

"I approached my administrator with the idea of hosting a film festival. My elementary school formed a committee comprised of teachers who liked to think outside of the box and weren't afraid to be wacky. We wanted to make our film festival experiential, so as families arrived, we had a puppet theater where they could play, a photo booth, a DJ spinning music, and silly questions to answer on video. The festival itself was scripted. We purposefully made the production very interactive to keep students' attention. Emcees hosted the show and provided transitions from one portion to the next, interspersing their talk with silly vignettes. We honored and recognized everyone we could, and the event was really well received by our school community. Throughout each year, when students knew their work could be shown in the school film festival and published on YouTube, they couldn't wait to create."

about prizes or awards. Rather, their value lies in hearing and seeing what young people have to say.

If public venues are intimidating or privacy policies too restrictive, consider hosting a classroom viewing party. Give students an opportunity to honor one another in recognition of the work they have invested in. One feedback or celebration model that I like to implement is Glows and Grows. Ask each person to provide one compliment and one constructive note for each movie they watch. Use sticky notes, a backchannel chat, or a Google Form (you can share the spreadsheet of responses with students after viewing has ended)—whatever method of comment collection works best for you. Taking the time to write comments as a class communicates respect for the student whose voice has been showcased. The practice of celebration adds another thread to the social fabric of storytelling.

Chapter 5

Integrating Moviemaking into the Curriculum

Moviemaking is undeniably standards-based. Not only does it build student capacity in the 4 C's (communication, collaboration, creativity, and critical thinking), but it can also be used for formative and summative assessment of student learning. The meaningful integration of digital storytelling relies on intelligent lesson design. Moviemaking can be efficiently implemented within the parameters of sequence and pacing guides, using limited technology resources, and can be employed in any content area, grade level, or educational setting.

Over the years, one recurring comment has consistently emerged whenever I facilitate professional development for teachers who are just beginning their storytelling journey: "Moviemaking is the perfect activity for after testing!" Many educators agree that high-stakes testing, though important, is not the be-all and end-all of instruction, yet we often treat it as such out of perceived neces-sity. Teachers who tend to "save" digital storytelling for the end of the year are doing a disservice to their students. This choice might be due, at least in part, to a lack of understanding about how to effectively address core content standards through moviemaking. Often, professional development in the area of educational technol-ogy is centered on tools, rather than pedagogy. Therefore, one of my goals for this book is to help teachers effectively plan units of study with moviemaking in mind.

Standards-Based Storytelling

Moviemaking in my classroom hinges on student expression of mastery pertaining to state-adopted content standards. Targeting multiple standards in one digital story is essential in order to maximize instructional time. Generally, it is beneficial to group together standards that would work well in a single project. If there is some kind of discernable overlap between related topics, it makes sense that a movie could address each area if properly planned and scaffolded.

Crafting digital stories through moviemaking addresses many different ISTE student standards as well—most notably, standard six, which is the Creative Communicator strand. It requires students to "communicate clearly and express themselves cre-atively for a variety of purposes using the platforms, tools, styles, formats, and digital media appropriate to their goals." In standard 6a, students focus on the stra-tegic use of digital tools to effectively communicate a message. This correlates to the use of video editing platforms, which contain many different tools and features that can be used to positive or negative effect, depending on the choices each student makes. Standard 6b requires students to create original content or remix existing content into new creations, while 6c focuses on students' ability to communicate complex ideas clearly using visuals or simulations. Finally, in order to meet standard 6d, students must publish or present for specific audiences. All of these Creative Communicator standards are inherent in the digital storytelling process.

Digital storytelling also has the potential to meet other ISTE student standards as well, particularly due to the amount of collaboration involved in the moviemaking process. Depending on how projects are structured, students can develop the Global Collaborator standards, as they work together with peers or community members to examine issues from multiple perspectives (7b). They might also leverage collaborative structures in order to function together as a team as they work toward a common goal (7c). Within the Innovative Designer strand, standard 4d focuses on how students develop the capacity to persevere through challenges as they work on open-ended projects. Because moviemaking is a task that allows for many different approaches, there is no one correct answer. Students have the opportunity to express their understanding in a way that is specific only to them. When coupled with content-area standards, the Knowledge Constructor strand of ISTE student standards is extremely applicable. Planning, researching, curating, connecting, and exploring ideas in pursuit of conclusions and solutions to problems—that is the essence of standards-based moviemaking.

Digital storytelling also naturally fosters student growth in the Digital Citizen strand, specifically when it comes to demonstrating an understanding for how to correctly use and share the property of others. Moviemaking relies on audio and visual media. Though students may film much of their own content, they will inevitably encounter situations in which they must leverage content created by others. Teaching students to respect the rights and obligations associated with intellectual property is instrumental to the production process. The degree to which each of these standards are built into a particular movie project depends on the teacher's lesson design.

Two Paths to Integration

From an instructional design standpoint, effective integration of moviemaking tends to fall into two different pathways: storytelling as a means to learn and storytelling as a capstone. Both styles of integration hold merit, so teachers must decide which model works best for their content area, age level, and curricular goals.

First, storytelling can be used to help students learn about a process or topic. Many STEM educators tend to gravitate toward this type of integration because of the hands-on nature of their subject areas. There are many opportunities for students to use moviemaking to document experiments, engineering challenges, and maker activities. It would be tempting to simply ask students to create a video version of their lab report with a recitation of steps and data, but that wouldn't really be storytelling. The story inherent in STEM movies revolves around a problem or challenge that must be solved. Emotional connection can be forged through a design thinking approach—students must examine a topic through the lens of empathy. Who are the people affected by the problem? Why should we care about finding a solution? What greater purpose is served by the work students are doing? These questions establish an emotional current and tension is generated through the search for a solution.

Georgia Terlaje, ELEMENTARY INSTRUCTIONAL COACH, FIFTH-GRADE TEACHER

"When I help other teachers plan moviemaking lessons, I encourage them to look through the lens of various crosscutting concepts in order to find inspiration for digital stories in science. Next Generation Science Standards discuss establishing a storyline throughout a unit of study, so that by the end of the unit you are able to tell the story of your learning. In the classrooms I work with, I use moviemaking as a touchpoint to assess student progress. For example, when children learn about food webs in fifth grade, they are learning the story of energy transfer. This means that they need to move beyond the basic knowledge of which animal eats another animal. From a more conceptual standpoint, the big idea really begins with the sun, which provides the energy that trickles down through the food chain. Since this is content that can be difficult for students to process, I ask them to create a digital story. Moviemaking is the perfect formative assessment, and students cherish the opportunity to be creative as they show their learning."

It should be noted that this type of integration requires a certain amount of fluidity in the moviemaking process. For example, before a science experiment begins, students should spend time planning their visuals in the form of a shot list. All of the required shots should be identified ahead of time so that students do not forget to document each of the steps in their learning process. Having a list ensures that asset collection is executed properly; otherwise, students may discover that they did not film everything they needed when they had the chance. In this situation, scriptwriting occurs *after* the visual planning and the recording; thus, the need for flexibility in the production process.

Teachers who use storytelling as a means to learn must structure content so that students are able to simultaneously construct understanding *and* document their thinking. Math teachers might ask their students to dissect a word problem then storify it in order to better connect academic content to the real world. In elementary, this can be done quite effectively using simple animation apps, such as Toontastic or Powtoon. Some of the best examples of STEM storytelling I have seen come from classrooms where students were given the opportunity to solidify their learning by making movies to teach others.

Another approach to moviemaking is to use storytelling as a capstone for learning. A capstone is a culminating project that exemplifies a student's learning experiences during a specific time—for example, during a unit of study. This is the method of integration that I have gravitated to consistently because it makes the most sense for how I teach and where I want moviemaking to fit into the instructional process. Moviemaking is the ultimate performance task. Often, there is a misconception that teachers must choose between rigorous academic tasks and creative tasks. When I talk to teachers who succumb to the idea of this forced choice, they generally cite restrictive sequence and pacing guides as their cause for concern. The reality is that creative tasks *are* rigorous and extremely academic in nature, particularly digital storytelling. Creativity and academics are not mutually exclusive; they can come together powerfully as the result of purposeful planning.

Teachers must begin by backwards mapping a unit of study. Identify the end result that students should be able to create, and then decide what learning needs to occur in order to make that product possible. Two questions guide the capstone planning process:

1. What will you need to teach in order to prepare students to share meaningful content?

2. What storytelling skills should students acquire alongside the content?

One of my favorite units is argumentative writing. A few years ago, I decided that I wanted my students to create collaborative public service announcements (PSAs) about the importance of coding and computer science in schools. During the course of the unit, students were required to synthesize information from multiple sources, construct a claim, support their claim with evidence, tailor their argument for a specific audience, and properly cite sources. Students also needed to understand how to create an effective PSA. All of these skills and concepts had to be woven together during the course of my unit plan.

To begin the instructional arc, students consumed multiple digital sources, both text and multimedia. They also collected direct quotes from these sources and generated anecdotal evidence by engaging in coding activities. Next, students collaboratively crafted claims to fit specific audiences (students, parents, or policy-makers) and categorized supporting evidence that would be convincing for each. A friend of mine happens to be a computer programmer, so students engaged in a video conference where they could ask questions and converse with a coding industry expert, which helped shape their idea of real-world relevance. Together, these experiences formed a deep well of knowledge from which students were able to draw as they began to create their PSAs.

To prepare for storytelling, we critically examined a variety of PSAs and talked about what persuasive approaches were effective. Students were excited to leverage this understanding as they prepared storyboards and planned video clips to film in order to illustrate their points. In the end, they were able to have authentic conversations about English content while also letting a creative task drive their learning. The finished PSAs expressed student mastery of argumentative writing in a more engaging fashion than traditional essay writing, making the learning sticky. Additionally, students were able to practice the important digital age skill of being able to craft and communicate a message clearly using technology.

Many of the teachers I have worked with ultimately gravitated toward integrating moviemaking as a capstone for several reasons. First, digital stories can reflect learning across multiple standards. Since a typical unit of study covers several standards, the end of a unit is a natural integration point for moviemaking. Second, many teachers find value in helping students develop storytelling skills—such as visual literacy, audio literacy, screen language, and video editing—slowly over time. Using short mini lessons spread over the course of several weeks or units is a manageable approach that works well when storytelling is used as a summative assessment of student learning. (Chapter 6 of this book outlines five essential mini lessons.) As you plan, remember that each of the projects contained in chapter 8 can be used as capstones.

Ricardo Flores, FIFTH-GRADE TEACHER

"Pedagogically, moviemaking ties into everything. My students create narratives on a wide variety of content—grammar, idioms, math problems, science. We write, draw, and tell stories about our learning, which gives voice to the kids who are really shy. There are some kids who are just deathly afraid to speak because of their language skills or personality. Moviemaking becomes the tool they use to show what they think, feel, and know. Those kids tend to be the most imaginative, because they just needed a key to unlock them—and that key is storytelling. It's not just something done for fun—it's academic. Student products demonstrate reading comprehension and subject matter proficiency. Essentially, movie projects are assessments. When you're trying to figure out how to integrate moviemaking, you need a rationale. Much like in any lesson plan, you need an objective and a way to assess that objective. Plan backwards with moviemaking in mind."

Interdisciplinary Collaboration

Moviemaking lends itself well to interdisciplinary collaboration. One year, my teaching partner and I worked together to help our students tell math-based digital stories. One of our students, Kimberly, was assigned to create a movie with the goal of communicating the algorithm for two-step equations. Of course, this needed to be done in story format, so Kimberly decided to tap into a memory from her real life: Her family wanted to visit her sick grandmother in Los Angeles and needed to purchase gas, but they weren't certain they would have enough money to fill their tank. Kimberly knew the cost of the gas and how much money was in her mother's wallet, and she needed to solve for the number of gallons of fuel that could be purchased. The story derived emotion from her family's desperate need to travel and the anxiety of potentially not having the means to make it to their destination. Kimberly actually filmed herself and her mother at the gas station down the street from the school. Her little brother sat inside the car, rolled down the backseat window, and propped a laptop on the windowsill to record them. At parent conferences that year, Kimberly's mom told me how moviemaking brought their family together and placed math at the center of their dinner table talk. My team partner reported that Kimberly demonstrated mastery of two-step equations on the district common assessment, and she taught her fifth-grade brother how to solve equations, too. Talk about learning that sticks!

Dr. Lee Grafton, FOURTH-GRADE TEACHER

"At the elementary level, co-planning is part of the fabric of many schools. When it comes to digital storytelling, and moviemaking in particular, working together as a grade level makes integration less intimidating. You have to be willing to think outside of the box—as in, what can I assess with moviemaking? If you can get buy-in from a whole grade level or subject area team, that can be powerful."

The success of interdisciplinary projects depends on careful co-planning. Teaching partners must determine which standards for each subject are met through the moviemaking process. Even if the content of the script overtly pertains to one subject matter, what other subject area standards are embedded? In Kimberly's example, the content was math-based, but the script writing connected more with Language Arts as students built and elaborated on ideas. My teaching partner and I had to decide where and when each stage of the moviemaking process would occur. Students ended up brainstorming in math class, writing scripts in Language Arts, obtaining feedback and collecting assets in math, and then editing during Language Arts. Daily communication with my teaching partner ensured that the process ran smoothly despite being spread between two classrooms.

Depth of Knowledge

Digital storytelling through moviemaking exemplifies deep learning. Norman Webb's Depth of Knowledge (DOK) Levels provide a frame of reference for how our students are engaging with content. It categorizes learning tasks according to the complexity of thought required to complete them. As we seek to ensure that we provide rigorous learning experiences for our students, it's important to understand where digital storytelling falls within the DOK framework. The bulk of storytelling tasks reside in levels 3 and 4, strategic and extended thinking. Depending on how lessons and storytelling tasks are planned, strategic thinking tasks generally include scripting, feedback, and critique. The creation of the story itself in terms of planning, asset collection, editing, and advanced critique are extended thinking tasks. Of note, any DOK Level 4 task must have multiple answers or approaches; they also frequently have multiple steps and result in multiple solutions. This is the deepest type of learning in which students can engage.

Repeated Attempts at Learning

Students' concept of storytelling builds over time; it is not a "one and done" type of activity. The more opportunities we can give kids to create movies, the more proficient they will become at storytelling through moviemaking. Over the years, I have discovered that the first movie students make takes longer than their second or third. It is worth it instructionally to allow for repeated attempts at learning. Creating lesson frames that can be reused with different content allows for process repetition. In part 3 of this book, you will find several quick-start project templates, such as the "I Am" poem. My students typically create several "I Am" movies within a single academic year (see figure 5.1). They go from taking five class periods to create their movie to producing a finished product in just two or three. Storytelling structures that are repeated reduce the cognitive load, thus allowing students to focus more on the content specific to that script, rather than on what it takes to write one. Building fluency with editing programs also helps streamline the process.

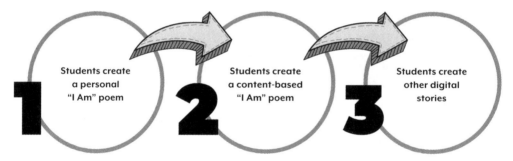

FIGURE 5.1

In elementary grades, repeated attempts at learning are especially important. So much of learning at young ages is built on repetition and routine. When digital storytelling is worked into the weekly schedule, students become quite proficient—both at storytelling *and* utilizing technology. One of the most impressive examples I have ever seen was on a site visit to a Southern California school whose staff I worked with through DIGICOM Learning. One of the TK-Kindergarten teachers had decided to use moviemaking as a way for students to practice their weekly vocabulary. The students utilized a class set of iPads with iMovie, and I remember watching in fascination as the little ones ran for the rainbow carpet to park themselves in front of their bright blue word chart. The teacher pointed at *gingerbread*, prompting students to open Safari, type the word, and navigate to images. They knew to tap and hold in order to save their favorite image on the iPad camera roll. Then, without help, students were able to import their images into iMovie and record voiceovers—all of this with the excited chatter of experience.

"Oh, look! We have the same gingerbread man, like in *Shrek*!" cried one student, pointing at the iPad the girl next to him was holding.

I remember being completely amazed as students manipulated the zoom feature to add animation to their images. When I asked the teacher what she had done to

Mario Cruz, HIGH SCHOOL ART TEACHER

"There is a progression to skills and the movie projects you plan for students. Typically, my students create three smaller movie projects before they get to the largest final project for the term. First, they analyze their own art and the steps they followed to create it. They focus on camera angles and narration for this piece, which brings their self-critique to life. The second movie project they undertake is a profile of art culture, for example, looking at the significance of symbols in art history. Again, they focus on voiceover, but they also add the collection of original footage filmed in the local art community. Finally, the third project students undertake is an interview. They interview one another and talk to each other about how art influences them. Not only do they engage in artistic discussion, but they also learn how to guide conversations during interviews and how to react and respond to what someone is telling them. We added the use of green screen during this project. All of this prepares students for their final digital story: a profile of a real-life local artist, including their work and their ideas about art. Students were well-equipped because they acquired all the skills they needed along the way."

accomplish such a well-oiled process, she smiled and said, "We do this every Friday, like clockwork." Thus, establishing routines makes the moviemaking process highly efficient in elementary classrooms.

Accessibility to Learning

Storytelling through moviemaking is accessible to all student groups, including reluctant writers, English language learners, and students with disabilities. The key to success for each of these populations is designing scaffolds that offer the right amount of support.

Students who struggle with writing often have trouble getting started. When confronted with an entirely open-ended project, they can feel intimidated or defeated before they even start brainstorming. For this reason, writing frameworks such as story spines or script templates are effective. These scaffolds allow students to begin the creative process from the zone of proximal development, meaning that there enough parameters in place to allow students to engage in the task. Confidence and comfort increase as reluctant writers find success.

English language learners and students with disabilities also benefit from the use of story spines and templates. Students who need support in writing clarity must receive explicit instruction in the area of transition words and phrases, which is exactly what a story spine provides. Sometimes the length of a storytelling task should be altered in order to accommodate student needs. Abbreviated templates are effective because they allow the student to focus on quality rather than quantity. A template can be abbreviated to whatever length the teacher believes is appropriate. One of the special education teachers I work with abbreviates the "I Am" poem template to as little as three lines for some of her students, while others receive a template containing six lines. There is plenty of room for differentiation depending on student needs. The progression of a story is really broken down into three parts. So, even a three-line template can mimic universal story structure (see table 5.1).

When presenting an abbreviated template to a student, however, it is important to allow room for the element of choice. Offering a "line bank" of alternative sentence frames and allowing students to switch out portions of their template at will keeps creative control in their hands.

TABLE 5.1 Abbreviated "I Am" Poem Template

Story Part	Abbreviated Lines	Alternative Lines
Introduction: What's the problem or challenge? What on-the-surface information must be shared?	I see _____.	I hear _____. I smell _____. I taste _____. I touch _____.
Building Emotional Tension: What events occur to build tension? What deeper information must be shared?	I understand _____.	I feel _____. I worry _____. I know _____. I want _____.
Resolution: What moment of revelation or resolution is achieved? What information is shared that looks toward the future?	I dream _____.	I hope _____. I wish _____. I pretend _____.

Sherry DiBari, SIXTH-GRADE TEACHER

"Moviemaking builds communication skills. For some of my bilingual students, who rarely speak English in class, having the opportunity to practice speaking was huge. The fact that they could write their thoughts down, then record as many times as needed in order to get their pronunciation correct, was empowering. They didn't have to get it right the first time or worry about being embarrassed in front of others."

Ricardo Flores, FIFTH-GRADE TEACHER

"Collaborative storytelling makes students with disabilities part of something special. Maybe a student struggles in a certain area, such as writing, but they can still articulate their ideas and contribute to a script. They might have tons of creativity and imagination and be able to map out what a story should look like. When working in collaborative groups, there are so many different tasks—researching, drawing, planning, filming, editing, sound selection. The wonderful thing is that there is a job for everybody, no matter who they are. Storytelling is very inclusive."

Making room for collaborative writing is also an effective strategy for high-needs students. The first attempt at an "I Am" poem project can be written as a whole group, while the second project cycle can then be approached in smaller groups, with a partner, or individually. The advantage to collaborative writing tasks is that it provides English learners with an opportunity to practice their language skills in an authentic environment. Scripted conversations certainly have their place in English language development. However, collaborative storytelling creates an opportunity for organic conversation, in which students are heavily invested. This type of dialogue fosters the use of both content-specific vocabulary and the transferrable lexicon of moviemaking.

An important point to remember is that scaffolds are meant to be removed as student competency grows, which requires teachers to be sensitive to how student needs change over time. One of my special education students, a quiet and shy middle-school girl, found a great affinity for storytelling. Initially, she used an abbreviated script template and worked with a small group of students so they could write together. For the second project cycle, however, she asked to write on her own because she felt more confident. By the end of the year, this student was utilizing a full-length script template and confidently creating work on par with grade-level expectations. All students can create compelling digital stories; some just need a bridge to help them get there.

— Feedback, Assessment, and Reflection —

Introducing rubrics early and often in the storytelling process helps students focus on how well their movie reflects what they have learned. I typically break rubric criteria into several categories: content, visual literacy, and audio literacy. Content is always weighted most heavily, in keeping with the standards-based nature of the task. However, visual and audio choices can also reflect content understanding, which is why they are addressed on rubrics I create.

The four-point rubric (table 5.2) is extremely detailed and effectively conveys the qualitative difference between movies that meet or exceed the mark and stories that do not. However, it is important to be mindful of the fact that four-point rubrics are text-intensive, making them less accessible to high-needs students or students for whom the concept of a rubric is relatively new. For this reason, I often gravitate toward one-point rubrics (see table 5.3). When providing feedback, best practice is to give specific, impactful comments about student work (Hattie & Timperley 2007).

Brandon Pack, ELEMENTARY SPECIAL EDUCATION TEACHER

"Storytelling is the ultimate accessibility tool. Students can listen to a text and demonstrate comprehension as they record a voice-over response and match it with images. This allows students to focus on content instead of the mechanics of writing, which can be an effective accommodation for some. Storytelling is also one of the best kinesthetic activities you can do with kids. They can get up and move as they film, even if it's just around the classroom. The hyperactive kids get to be the center of attention, shy kids can have a creative outlet, and you don't have to teach every skill to every kid. You can customize your instruction of these skills to the roster of kids you teach based on their strengths. Everyone can have a job, just like a real film set. In storytelling, there is a place for everyone."

The format of a one-point rubric fosters specificity, allowing teachers to help students understand what they are doing well and what needs improvement. It is also important to limit feedback so that it is not overwhelming. Start by providing guidance on big-picture issues pertaining to content, while also identifying one or two storytelling areas that need work. For example, if a student has multiple audio and visual errors in their editing, focus on the one area that most impacts the story of their learning as a whole.

TABLE 5.2 Sample Four-Point Rubric for Moviemaking

	Excellent	Adequate	Incomplete
Quality of Information	The script relates a variety of personal details about the life of the author. Sensory, creative language is used. The student shares **meaningful** information and chooses words carefully. An advanced level of vocabulary is used.	The script relates some personal details about the life of the author, but there is not a wide variety. Some sensory, creative language is used. The student shares mostly meaningful information, although word choice was not careful. An advanced level of vocabulary is NOT used.	The script relates a few personal details about the life of the author, but there is not much variety. Little or no sensory, creative language is used. The student shares some meaningful information, but word choice was not careful. An advanced level of vocabulary is NOT used.
Quality of Video Clips	All of the movie is made up of high-definition video clips or images. All video was filmed in **LANDSCAPE** mode or the "blur background" tool was used.	Most of the movie is made up of high-definition video clips or images. Most of the video was filmed in **LANDSCAPE** mode, and/or the "blur background" tool was used some of the time.	There are no high-definition video clips or images. Some of the video clips were filmed in **PORTRAIT** mode or the "blur background" tool was NOT used at all.

	Excellent	Adequate	Incomplete
Agreement	All of the video clips perfectly match the subject that is being talked about in the voiceover. Every time the subject of the voiceover changes, the image changes. There are no cartoon images, no images of words, and no blurry images.	Most of the video clips match the subject that is being talked about in the voiceover. However, the video clips may not be the BEST clips to communicate what is being said. There are no cartoon images, no images of words, and only one or two blurry images.	The video clips do not match the subject that is being talked about in the voiceover. Clips change at random. There are cartoon images, images of words, and/or blurry images.
Voiceover	The voiceover is loud, clear, and easy to hear. The speaker pronounces words correctly. The voiceover is balanced to be the **LOUDEST** audio track in the project. The voice can be heard very clearly over the music or sound effects. There is **ZERO** background noise.	The voiceover is somewhat clear but may not be quite loud enough. The speaker pronounces most words correctly. The voiceover is balanced to be the **LOUDEST** audio track in the project. The voice can be heard very clearly over the music or sound effects. There is not much, if any, background noise.	The voiceover is **NOT** clear or easy to hear. The speaker pronounces some words incorrectly. The voiceover is **NOT** balanced to be the loudest audio track in the project. The voice cannot be heard very clearly over the music or sound effects. There is background noise.
Music	The music track fades in, fades out, and does not overpower the speaker's voice. The music is copyright-free and downloaded from a copyright-free source.	The music track is present. The music track does NOT fade in or fade out. The music might not be copyright-free, and it might not be downloaded from a copyright-free source.	There is no music track.

continued

	Excellent	Adequate	Incomplete
Transitions and Effects	Transitions and effects are used wisely. The student clearly matched transitions with appropriate word choice in the script. If effects are present, they are not distracting.	Transitions and effects are mostly used wisely. The student somewhat matched transitions with appropriate word choice in the script. Effects are not used well and might be distracting.	The student did not use transitions or used them poorly. The student may have used too many effects that were very distracting.
Attention to Detail	Editing strategies are effective, including appropriate sequencing and trimming of clips, cohesive stylistic choices (filters, FX, text, colors, etc.), and economy of detail. Text contains no errors.	Editing strategies are somewhat effective, including appropriate sequencing and trimming of clips, cohesive stylistic choices (filters, FX, text, colors, etc.), and economy of detail. Text contains few errors.	Editing strategies are inconsistent and/or lacking, including appropriate sequencing and trimming of clips, cohesive stylistic choices (filters, FX, text, colors, etc.), and economy of detail. Text contains many errors.
Animation	Animation is used to draw attention to important aspects of images and videos. There is a variety of "push" or "pull" techniques.	Animation is used, but it is not used purposefully. There is little variety of "push" or "pull" techniques.	Animation is not used at all.

TABLE 5.3 Sample One-Point Rubric for Moviemaking

CONCERNS	CRITERIA	ACHIEVEMENTS
Areas That Need Work	**Standards for this Performance**	**Evidence of Meeting or Exceeding Standards**
	Content: Student developed a claim.	
	Content: Student cited 3–5 pieces of specific evidence to support their claim.	
	Content: Student created the PSA for a specific, discernable audience (e.g., parents, teachers, students, policymakers).	
	Audio Literacy: Student recorded a clear voiceover with expression and appropriate pacing.	
	Visual Literacy: Student followed the concept of agreement, meaning that audio, text, and supporting visuals match in content where appropriate.	

Research indicates that when people are provided immediate feedback on their work, their performance shows a larger increase than those whose feedback is delayed (Opitz et al., 2011). Often, the feedback process can be slow when students must turn in their work, wait for teachers to grade it, then wait to receive a copy of the rubric containing written feedback. Student-teacher collaborative evaluation is one way to ensure that feedback is provided in a timely fashion. As students finish their movies, I choose to sit down with them for a one-on-one conference. Though this may sound like a time-intensive task, it is easily accomplished using the station rotation model of blended learning. Conferences occur at a teacher-led station and five to six conferences are conducted within a 20-minute time frame. Thus, all students receive personalized feedback in two periods. Together, we assess the quality of their movie, consulting the rubric together and noting our observations about what was accomplished effectively and what still needs work. Often, students are able to clarify their thinking, which helps me gain a better picture about what type of help I need to provide in order to bridge any gaps in understanding. This collaborative evaluation also provides a perfect opportunity for students to ask questions. The overall effect of these conferences is the development of a close-knit storytelling community, wherein feedback is valued for continued growth as storytellers.

Having the ability to think about and reflect on work is an important life skill for students to develop. There are many positive correlations between learning communities and the growth of metacognitive skills. One study found that metacognition increases when classroom-based learning communities use self-assessment. Students were able to identify their own strengths and weaknesses, which then led to self-regulation demonstrated by planning, monitoring, and reflection (Siegesmund 2016). Consequently, whenever student-teacher collaborative evaluation is not possible, I still ask students to assess their work using the rubric. This type of metacognition helps students think about their work on a long-term trajectory. Rather than seeing a digital story as a one-time project for which they receive a grade and move on, students consider what storytelling strengths they must continue to exercise, as well as which skills they need to acquire or refine.

Chapter 6
Storytelling Mini Lessons

In cooking, there is the concept of mise en place. Literally translated from French, it means "set in place," and refers to portioning ingredients into small bowls before one begins to cook. Having the ingredients measured and organized ahead of time streamlines the cooking process and ensures that all of the components needed for the creation of a delicious dish are present. Similarly, teachers must determine how best to mete out movie-making skill development in order to help their students tell effective stories. Audiovisual skills that are taught and reinforced over time become transferrable between content areas as students learn to communicate clearly in a digital medium. Rather than asking students to become expert moviemakers all at once, essential skills can be taught via mini lessons alongside core content throughout the course of a unit.

This chapter outlines five key mini lessons teachers can use with their students. Some of the lessons build screen grammar, while others deal with more technical aspects of moviemaking. Screen grammar, also called film grammar, refers to the terms that are specific to filmmaking, such as the difference between a frame and a scene. Some of the most important components of screen grammar are the various film angles. Knowing the proper terms for these angles facilitates collaborative conversations between students, as well as dialogue and feedback between teachers and students. Essential technical aspects of movie-making include learning how to appropriately match audio and visual components, as well as how to record compelling voiceovers. It is also important that students understand how to effectively leverage the Ken Burns effect, a push-and-pull animation sometimes applied to still photos. Finally, having and using a common lexicon to discuss cinematic elements necessitates the use of the SCALE acronym, which will also be covered in this chapter.

Film Angle Mini Lesson and Extension Activities

The first mini lesson explains the four basic film angles: wide, medium, close-up, and over-the-shoulder. Wide shots are used to communicate the setting, where characters may appear in the shot, but are depicted with plenty of scenery context to help viewers place the action. This type of shot is essential at the beginning of a scene to establish the setting. Establishing shots are one of the most frequently forgotten when students collect assets, whether filming or locating existing resources. Medium shots show much less of the setting than wide clips. The point is to shift the viewer's focus away from the setting to focus more on the character(s). Shots build understanding, so the overall objective is to reveal more information with each shot that appears. Close-up shots are used to showcase important objects or character reactions—another shot that often students seem to forget to include. Finally, the over-the-shoulder shot is used to depict conversations between characters. This type of shot also allows the viewer to observe what a character is seeing, so if the story hinges on some important information the character sees, the viewer will see it along with them. The goal of the film angle mini lesson is to help students identify these angles and begin to consider how they might be used together to unveil settings, characters, and conflict.

First, find a movie trailer that students will be interested in watching. Listen to their conversations to find out what is currently popular or pay attention to social media. You can even ask students for suggestions—just make sure you preview each trailer before

using it in order to make sure the content is appropriate for your grade level. Show students the trailer, which usually lasts 1–2 minutes. Ask them to pay attention to how the camera moves. Then, ask students to divide a piece of paper into quadrants using a pencil or pen. You could also allow them to use a drawing app on a tablet, or a whiteboard with a marker. Generally, I ask students to use their interactive notebooks, so storytelling notes are stored alongside content area notes. Spend 5–6 minutes drawing simple sketches to illustrate each of the four basic film angles. Talk to students about how and why each angle is used. When students volunteer ideas, offer validation and treat the sketching time as a conversation. After each of the four angles have been covered, replay the movie trailer and pause it randomly. Each time the video pauses, ask students to shout out the film angle that appears. By the end of the trailer, student accuracy will be extremely high. This entire mini lesson should take approximately 10 minutes—certainly no more than 15. The point is to give a bite-size skill lesson that can be further developed throughout the rest of the week.

FIGURE 6.1 Sample drawings of the four film angles taught during the Film Angle Mini Lesson.

For the next several days, ask students to practice their film angle literacy using a film angle sorting task as a warm-up (see Figure 6.2). Students work together in pairs to sort of variety of images into categories labeled with the four basic film angles. You can utilize screenshots from popular movies, pictures you have taken yourself, or photos students submit. For each sorting task, include 8–10 images for students to identify; each task takes approximately 2–3 minutes total, including partner discussion.

DOWNLOAD THE GOOGLE DRAW FILM ANGLES SORTING ACTIVITY

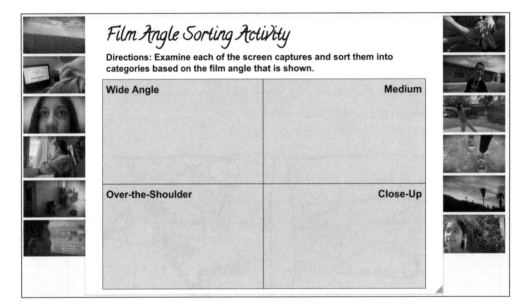

Film Angle Sorting Activity

Directions: Examine each of the screen captures and sort them into categories based on the film angle that is shown.

Wide Angle	Medium
Over-the-Shoulder	**Close-Up**

FIGURE 6.2 The Google Draw sorting activity for the Film Angle Mini Lesson.

Another engaging follow-up to this mini lesson is tasking students with a film angle scavenger hunt. Form teams of two or three and give students a list of shots to collect. Have someone on each team take pictures using a phone, a classroom tablet, a Chromebook, or the like. Offering a prize can give a powerful incentive, but often just the sight of seconds ticking by on a timer on the board provides ample motivation. The timer creates impetus to finish quickly, so this follow-up exercise generally takes 5 minutes or less.

Anyone who has studied film or performed a quick internet search likely knows that there are more than four film angles. Typically, I do not instruct these angles and prefer to let students discover them on their own instead. Students will absolutely begin to move their cameras in new ways and organically discover how to communicate visual information even more effectively. The four basic angles simply form a baseline understanding.

Agreement Mini Lesson

Agreement refers to when audio and visual components match. This is a difficult skill for students to acquire, because they often take a word association approach to editing when a more literal approach is required. For several years, I took my classes to visit the local news station, and the director shared that the concept of agreement is explained as "see dog, say dog" in the news industry. Since it is easy to remember, I often teach this phrase to my students. From a storytelling standpoint, agreement is much more than just matching the topic of a voiceover with an appropriate image. Over time, agreement also becomes about matching the mood or tone and conveying the most information possible. Some images are more powerful than others—finding the exact right image to communicate both on-the-surface and under-the-surface meaning is an essential storytelling skill.

For this 10-minute mini lesson, I begin by telling students to find a picture of the "best dog ever." I set a one-minute timer and students begin wildly searching through Google Images, each trying to find the cutest dog, or the dog most like their own, or just a dog that looks like one they would want to adopt. I ask students to open their image in a new tab and tell their partners why the dog they found is the best. A few students share out to the whole class, after which I ask them to consider two pictures of a yellow dog. In one picture, the dog is standing on grass looking off camera. In the other picture, the dog is captured mid-run, jaws gaping, as he lunges toward a tennis ball that is just out of reach. Next comes the all-important question: Which image tells a better story? Student hands shoot into the air, and everyone

inevitably agrees that the dog chasing the ball is in the middle of
a story. Responses vary and tend to get more entertaining as the
conversation progresses. Maybe the dog's owner threw the ball.
Maybe the ball was knocked over a fence and the dog is retrieving
it. Maybe the ball is the dog's favorite and it is about to roll over a
cliff into the sea! Maybe the ball is rolling toward a mouse village
and the dog is the superhero who will save them!

**DOG VIDEO FOR
AGREEMENT LESSON**

From there, I ask students to reprise their initial task. Find a picture of the best dog
ever *and* make sure the picture tells a story. The timer is set for two minutes, and
usually you can hear a pin drop because students are so focused on finding the best
possible dog with the best possible story to share. After the timer, students turn to
their partners to show their pictures and tell their stories. Be prepared—your classroom will get loud as excited student voices share the images they found.

The final step is to show students how video can sometimes add a little something
extra, a sensory layer that makes a subject even more compelling. Students view
a YouTube video I found on social media a few years ago (see the QR code on this
page). Someone strapped a GoPro camera onto a dog's back and then unleashed
him at the top of a rocky hill leading down to a beach. The entire clip is filmed from
the dog's perspective, as he runs joyously down the embankment and rushes headfirst into the waves. There is a moment where the dog is suspended in a midair leap
before dipping below the surface of the water, and that is usually about the time the
whole class sighs longingly and someone inevitably says, "I wish we had an ocean
here in our desert."

This entire instructional sequence should take approximately 10 minutes, definitely
no more than 15. The goal was to teach students to think about the story that an
individual image can tell. With this foundational understanding, students will be
able to select better, more powerful images for their digital stories.

This is also a good time to teach students how to use the advanced search tools to
filter for images that are high-resolution and copyright-free (see figure 6.3). If you
are unfamiliar with how to conduct an advanced image search, navigate to Google

Images and search for your topic. Click on the Tools button, then select the desired size. Large images are always best because they are the highest resolution. Images are measured in pixels, so the higher the pixel count, the higher the resolution. When images appear blurry, it is because they have a low pixel count. Google displays the pixel measurements for each image, which is extremely helpful for students. Another advanced search tool allows users to filter images according to their Creative Commons license. Whenever students use images from the web, it is important to ensure they are following copyright and giving credit through proper citation. Digital citizenship skills are especially important if work is to be shared beyond classroom walls. Thus, explicitly teaching students to search for images that are free to use and share is essential.

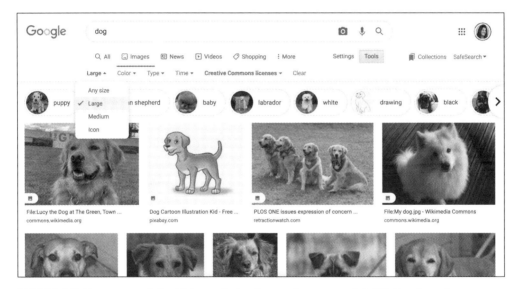

FIGURE 6.3 How to search for high-resolution images is an essential skill. Teach students to toggle the search settings and select search criteria for large images only.

Audio Fluency Mini Lessons

Many of the movie projects my students undertake rely on a voiceover. In fact, most of the quick-start lesson frames contained in part 3 of this book include voiceovers as their primary audio component. Most students are not immediately aware of the impact a voiceover can have on their digital story. There are many aspects of voice recording to be aware of, including but not limited to background noise, ambient noise, pacing, intonation, pronunciation, and expression. Other layers of sound also play a part in digital stories, such as music and sound effects.

One of the challenges of recording audio is the presence of background noise. Whether in the classroom or at home, there are generally lots of other voices that can be accidentally captured in the recording process. There are also many sources of ambient noise, such as air conditioners, fans, cooking food, footsteps, or even wildlife. In the desert where my students and I live, cicadas are particularly loud during certain times of the year. Students are hard-pressed to find anywhere outside the classroom that does not offer refuge to these loud bugs, making cicada-free spots golden.

Voice recording also requires rehearsal, because lines must be delivered with expression at an appropriate pace. In talking with some of my students over the years, simply pressing the Record button causes enough anxiety that they tend to rush through all of their words using little inflection. So, giving students opportunities to practice is key. Even if a voiceover is recorded perfectly, its storytelling potential can still be destroyed by the heavy-handed use of sound effects or musical choices that simply do not "agree" (that is, do not match up) with the mood, tone, or subject matter.

Since there are so many audio pitfalls to avoid, I decided to ask students to create the worst possible audio track for a 20-second digital story. This idea was inspired by Marlena Hebern and Jon Corippo, authors of *The EduProtocol Field Guide* (2018). They published a lesson frame in their first field guide that required students to create the worst possible presentation using software of their choice. In a similar fashion, I ask my students to create truly awful audio in order to help them understand what absolutely does *not* work when it comes to storytelling. Students are provided with a short script and given 10 minutes to record an audio track with as much background and ambient noise as possible. Students read as fast or as slow as they can using intonation that absolutely does not match the content. Students then add ill-suited music and whatever sound effects they can find, taking an "everything and the kitchen sink" approach. One of my favorite student projects of all time featured a student who decided to read as slowly as possible. The script was a paragraph featuring what was meant to be an exciting action sequence. Instead, the student carried his Chromebook over to record next to the oscillating fan in one corner of our classroom. He borrowed the pacing and intonation of the teacher played by Ben Stein in *Ferris Bueller's Day Off* and added a bunch of nature sound effects. The end result was a mixture of the other students reading in the background, the whir of the fan, the dead tones of his own voice, sappy music, and rainforest sounds. It was absolutely hysterical to listen to! Students share their recordings with a partner and the giggles make this mini lesson worth it. They also totally grasp what *not* to do by the end of their awful recordings.

The second 10-minute mini lesson that follows is an opportunity for redemption. Now that students know what to avoid, they must recreate their recording using best practices. This time, students record using earbuds with a microphone to focus their voices. They avoid background noise by spreading out and stay away from air conditioners and fans. They read using an appropriate pace and tone, adding expression where needed. At this point, paying attention to music and the mood it creates becomes almost second nature, and sound effects are relevant. My favorite feature about these two connected audio mini lessons is that students are able to discover on their own what makes or breaks an audio recording—no boring teacher lecture needed!

Ken Burns Effect Mini Lesson

The Ken Burns effect refers to the movement of the camera as it pans or zooms across a still photo. This type of push-and-pull animation adds life to an otherwise static image. The technique was honed by Ken Burns, an American filmmaker widely known for his use of historical images in documentary films, and has become so ubiquitous that it is sometimes automatically applied by movie-editing software. It is important to teach students to retain control over the use of animation, because purposeful choices of when exactly to apply the Ken Burns effect can greatly improve the overall quality of a movie.

To teach this 10-minute mini lesson, I simply show students how to access the push-and-pull animation tools. On iMovie, the tool is called Ken Burns, while on WeVideo's browser-based software, it is called Animation. The iOS version of iMovie has a plus and minus feature in the corner of the preview box that allows users to set a start and stop point for zoom animation. Adobe Spark, Animoto, and other online editing software contain static zoom features. Once students know where to locate the animation tools, it's just a matter of letting them play. To wrap up this hands-on exploration, I typically show students an anchor movie that uses the Ken Burns effect to enhance the overall message of the story. You can always use a video clip from an actual Ken Burns documentary, but I find it is more impactful to use student-created work, which is part of the reason I archive so many movie projects on our classroom YouTube channel. Targeted viewing can be an incredible tool. When we give students something specific to focus on, such as paying attention to how the storyteller used the Ken Burns effect, students are able to form a better understanding from the viewing experience.

These guiding questions can help facilitate classroom discussion:

1. How did zooming in on an image help the storyteller communicate their message?

2. What effect did panning across an image create?

3. How do you think this movie would have been different without the use of animation?

SCALE Mini Lessons

As previously discussed, developing a common lexicon of moviemaking and storytelling terms can prove enormously helpful in the classroom. During my tenure as a teacher consultant at DIGICOM Learning in Palm Springs, the curriculum team worked out an acronym to help students and teachers understand the various elements that comprise movies: SCALE. The letters of SCALE stand for Story, Camera, Audio, Look, and Editing. High-quality digital stories exhibit best practices in most (if not all) of these categories. Though this acronym was originally developed to help teachers and students improve their movies by "scaling them up" to the next level, I found it most useful to use SCALE as a pre-teaching and critical viewing tool.

If we want students to create better movies, we need to orchestrate as many opportunities as possible for them to watch and appreciate the work of other young people. Even though students consume an unprecedented amount of media through streaming services and social media platforms, they are not necessarily used to seeing their peers create cinematic content. Watching and discussing that content using common language can be enlightening.

As this book has discussed extensively, the essence of moviemaking is the development of an emotionally impactful story that resonates. When evaluating the element of **Story**, I ask students to determine whether the action unfolds in three parts. Remember, though some might refer to this as beginning, middle, and end, it is really more about emotional beats. Students must also be able to analyze whether a story is compelling, with evidence to support why it is or is not. Finally, students need to assess whether economy of detail was applied by the person who created the movie. Generally, storytellers show instead of telling. The art is to show just enough for viewers to grasp what is occurring, rather than belaboring the point. Every teacher who has ever made a movie with students knows what it is like to watch an extended cut of a character walking down the hallway during a 15-second take. The scripting equivalent might be including too much detail when less would suffice.

When evaluating **Camera**, students should pay attention to the number and types of film angles used. Whether images are clear or pixelated is a consideration when using photos as opposed to video footage. As previously mentioned, students are prone to leaving two particular types of shots out of their work: close-ups to show character reactions and establishing shots. Reaction shots are important because they visually inform the viewer about how certain events or pieces of information are received by the characters. They also trigger emotion in the audience, so leaving out a reaction shot can significantly lessen the emotional resonance of a scene. Establishing shots show the setting of a scene and help viewers understand the larger context in which the action occurs. Usually, students like to cut straight to the action, as opposed to taking a few seconds to set the stage for the audience. I teach my students to pay particular attention to how and when others integrate these two types of shots. If students know to look for them, they are more likely to include them in their own work.

Students need to be able to assess **Audio** in terms of balance. Audio fluency is important and, once achieved, should not be undermined by inappropriately balanced supporting tracks. New storytellers have a tendency to drop music and sound effects into the audio, but then forget to turn them down during voiceovers or dialogue. Some editing software balances automatically (this tool is sometimes referred to as "ducking"), but most require manual manipulation. Choosing music purposefully so that it evokes emotion is key; this is a skill that must be explicitly taught, so it helps to have recurring conversations about the effect of music on mood and tone.

When evaluating the **Look** of a movie, students should consider the physical setting. Understanding basic lighting concepts, such as whether faces are properly illuminated or if there is backlighting, can greatly improve the footage students are able to capture. Additionally, students should pay attention to their surroundings. Though actual set design is definitely beyond the scope of what we do in the core content classroom, we *can* teach our students to film in locations that are as distraction-free as possible. Nothing ruins a scene more than seeing other students filming in the background!

Look is closely connected to **Editing** because the two elements work hand in hand. The use of transitions can either add to or distract from the story, and the amount of precision used when editing can affect a story's pace. For example, live-action clips should be trimmed so that angles flow seamlessly from one shot to the next. The editing stage is when economy of detail comes into play on a second-by-second basis. Every frame of a movie should contribute to the story; if it does not contribute, it should be cut. Students become excellent editors when they have

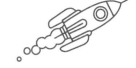

multiple opportunities to see what good editing looks like from work their peers have produced.

TABLE 6.1 SCALE Guiding Questions

Story	Does the story have three parts (emotional beats)?
	Is the story compelling?
	Is there economy of detail?
Camera	Are a variety of angles used?
	Are images clear or pixelated?
	Did you include establishing shots?
Audio	Are voiceovers and music balanced?
	Does the voiceover have expression?
	Does the music evoke emotion?
Look	Is there backlighting?
	Are faces properly illuminated?
	Did you choose a distraction-free location?
Editing	Did you use precision when editing?
	Do transitions add or distract?
	Does every frame help tell a story?

An effective 10- to 15-minute mini lesson that can be repeated often is a SCALE Viewing Party. Organize students into groups of five and give each person in the group a SCALE card. Each card consists of a letter from the SCALE acronym and a series of guiding questions (see table 6.1) pertaining to that particular aspect of moviemaking. If students are working in groups of four, then combine both the Look and Editing categories by giving both of these cards to one person. Select a student-created movie to watch and then discuss as a whole class using the prompts on the SCALE cards. This gives teachers the opportunity to both model (by thinking aloud) and facilitate (by engaging the point of view of several outspoken students).

It is important that students understand what a critical viewing discussion sounds like before they try it on their own.

DOWNLOAD SCALE CARDS

When the class is ready, watch a second student-created movie and have students discuss in their small groups. Ask each group to document their discussion using a piece of poster paper and a maker. Hang the papers on the wall or have one person from each group hold them up. Ask students to draw general conclusions based on common observations they see recorded on the group posters. A variation of this activity is to establish groups to evaluate each element of SCALE, one group assessing story, another group assessing audio, etc. Groups can record their observations on a Padlet wall, poster paper, or via backchannel chat.

The SCALE mini lesson can be repeated throughout the year. It can also be applied during small group feedback sessions as a way to evaluate first drafts. Once students have internalized the SCALE acronym, they are better able to view and discuss their own work as well as the work of their peers.

Julie Barda, SEVENTH-GRADE TEACHER

"Every movie project I ask my students to create has a metacognitive component. We go through the process in stages, with multiple stopping points, so that students have opportunities to reflect and improve their work. Even all the way up to the end of the storytelling process, after they have turned in their final draft, I always ask them: *If I gave you another day, what would you change? What would you make better?* In this way, they realize that their stories are never really done, per se. There is a constant back-and-forth of ideas resulting from reflection. Dissecting their work and the work of others makes students better writers and editors."

Chapter 7

Removing Barriers from Storytelling

As a California Teacher of the Year and an advocate for digital storytelling in core content areas, I have been fortunate to visit many classrooms, speak with many teachers, and provide professional development in a variety of venues. One of the most striking things I've realized is that, as a whole, we simply do not give our students enough opportunities to tell digital stories. When asked what keeps them from allowing their students to create movies, teachers have identified three main barriers: time, technology, and truth.

TIME	TECHNOLOGY	TRUTH
"It's difficult to fit digital storytelling into my curriculum. I've got a sequence and pacing guide to follow, and I just can't afford to lose weeks at a time."	*"I don't have enough devices for each student. I'm also not great at video editing programs. I'm worried I won't know how to help my students."*	*"I don't know how to get my students to tell worthwhile stories. How do you get them to say something personal and meaningful?"*

FIGURE 7.1

Finding Time for Moviemaking

One of my favorite ways to open a weeklong professional development series is to facilitate a speed-greeting icebreaker activity. Participating teachers arrange their chairs into two lines, so that each person is facing a partner. Pairs then have two minutes to introduce themselves, talk about their storytelling experience, and identify the single largest barrier that keeps them from making more movies in their classroom. After each two-minute exchange, everyone in one row shifts over one chair and the speed greeting begins again. Overwhelmingly, across at least a dozen exchanges in every workshop, the number one response teachers provide is feeling like there is never enough time.

Teachers absolutely have very full plates. As a teacher who is currently in the trenches, I understand that time is a valuable commodity in short supply. When I first began making movies with students, I would set aside a solid seven to ten days to be able to write and film all original content and move through the entire production process, start to finish. Other teachers I encountered did that too, so it took me

a while to question whether that was my only option. Most of the other storytelling teachers I met at conferences taught media classes or electives, so time was not as much of an issue. The sequence and pacing of their courses depended almost entirely on their own professional judgment, unlike the core classes I taught.

The initial solution I found involved treating moviemaking as a capstone for learning. A capstone experience is defined as a culminating project that is multifaceted and serves as an expression of learning after engaging in a unit of study. I have used all of the projects contained in chapter 8 as capstones, as have many of the educators who have been profiled in this book—both elementary *and* secondary. By addressing multiple standards throughout a unit and teaching storytelling mini lessons along-side content as described in chapters 5 and 6, I was able to build many chances for students to create digital stories as a showcase for their mastery. In other words, movies became a form of assessment.

As educators, we need to shift our thinking in terms of how we view moviemaking. The main piece of advice I provide teachers from all grade levels is this: Moviemaking *is not* something we do in addition to everything else. Moviemaking *is* a manifestation of student learning. Therefore, as we plan lessons with the end in mind, we need to redesign how we choose to measure student understanding. Teachers make plenty of time for multiple-choice tests and projects. What would happen if they removed some of those and simply allocated that time for standards-based moviemaking instead? When thought leaders talk about redefining what learning looks like within the walls of our classrooms, this is the type of transformation that exemplifies that sentiment.

In addition, teachers should carefully consider the scope of the moviemaking projects they ask their students to undertake. Often, we tend to buy in to the idea that a longer movie is better because it exhibits more effort and time investment. However, project length is not at all indicative of quality; rather, it is the writing and execution of audiovisual literacy concepts that speaks to students' skills. While a three- to five-minute movie project doesn't sound terribly long on paper, it is nearly overwhelming in terms of production time. Thus, most of the movie projects I design result in a finished product that is two minutes or less—and sometimes as short as

15 seconds! David Vogel once told me that any story worth telling can be told in two minutes. After so many years making movies with students, I can vouch for the veracity of his statement. So, whenever possible, I try to guide my students in exercising economy of detail.

Perhaps the most beneficial time-saving strategy I have adopted is an inverted model of instruction. My middle school English Language Arts classes are blended, using a station rotation model three days each week. Students visit several stations per day and complete the tasks at each station within the twenty-minute time frame given for each. Some of the tasks are individual and some are collaborative; one station is always teacher-led and provides an opportunity for small group instruction. When entering the production process of moviemaking, stations are an effective

Frank Guttler, DIGITAL STORYTELLING INTEGRATION COACH

"The second and third grade teachers that I work with have a farm-to-table and sustainability unit that currently exists within their language arts and science curriculum. It involves research and experiential learning, during which students grow tomatoes in the school garden. Teachers also usually take their students to a farmer's market to meet local farmers and explore the types of food they produce. As a team, we decided to embed digital storytelling as a way to document student learning throughout this unit. Before our trip to the market, I created a template for students to use in order to write short scripts. They even brainstormed the types of shots they wanted to capture since we had previously covered a few basic film angles. On the day of our trip, students utilized iPads to film. Their efforts were purposeful because they had carefully planned everything out. Back in the classroom, we edited our footage together with voiceovers to tell the story of our trip to the market, and students were able to produce some wonderful products to share their learning. This illustrates how digital storytelling can fit into the schedule alongside what teachers already do. It both enhances and enriches curriculum, while offering a personalized experience for every student."

way to integrate storytelling tasks, from collecting images or audio files to recording a voiceover or making progress on editing. I have used my teacher-led station for small group collaborative writing or for feedback on scripts or first draft edits (see table 7.1 for suggested storytelling stations). The work of Dr. Catlin Tucker helped me improve my practice (Tucker, 2019), and I credit the station rotation model for enabling students to create many storytelling projects in one year.

TABLE 7.1 Station Rotation Storytelling Tasks

Preproduction Tasks	Production Tasks	Postproduction Tasks
Research	Collecting images or audio files	Editing
Collaborative or individual writing using script templates	Recording voiceovers	First draft feedback from peers or teacher
Creating storyboards or two-column notes	Filming original video clips to intersperse with existing visual resources	Developing a revision plan for a second draft
Script feedback from peers or teacher		Self-assessment and reflection

In elementary classrooms, there are several ways teachers can undertake moviemaking with their students. Often, subjects are framed as a series of units of study, so the idea of moviemaking as a capstone project can work in elementary classrooms as well. Some of the teachers I have worked with have indicated that language arts and math instruction tend to be highly regimented, both in terms of instructional minutes and required pacing, so they have most often found opportunities for storytelling associated with science and social studies instead. There are also pockets of the day that are left to teacher discretion, such as designated English Language Development (ELD) time. During this portion of the schedule, students are leveled into groups based on language proficiency, so it is natural that each group requires a different approach pertaining to pace and scaffolds. Moviemaking contains many opportunities to practice speaking skills, which most ELD students need. Added to that is the element of recording one's voice while reading scripts; many teachers have found that asking students to listen to their audio playback as a means to identify errors has proven an invaluable strategy for improvement.

Dr. Lee Grafton, FOURTH-GRADE TEACHER

"In my classroom, we use digital storytelling through movie-making during our designated ELD time. I prefer to use this time because it is without pacing constraints; I can focus on a specific group and spend as much time as I want. For one rotation, we learned about a force and motion and the students' capstone project was to create a movie. Since this was the first time that students were creating, I provided the script for them as an anchor text. We dissected the script together, looking at its parts and how the information was structured as a short narrative. Students then recorded the anchor script as their own and edited everything together, which reduced the cognitive load of the task, allowing them to learn *how* to make a movie to showcase learning. For the next rotation, we did a social studies unit on California history and students wrote their own scripts. Since they already understood what a well-written script should look like, they were able to write confidently. In fact, they were really good!"

Using moviemaking lesson frames that can be repeated as content changes has been a time-saver as well. A student's first attempt at a project is much slower than their second, third, or fourth. Building storytelling fluency reduces the time needed to create, which takes pressure off teachers' pacing guides. The first time my students create a project can take up to five partial class periods, but by the time we hit our stride with the second or third project, students only need three periods to create. Keep in mind that any of the script templates for the projects in chapter 8 can be pared down to suit your students' needs.

Shifting away from having students film all original content for their movies was an important time-saving step for my classroom. When students are able to utilize existing resources, the asset collection phase is cut in half. For younger grades, it can save a lot of time when teachers populate a shared folder full of images pertaining to a specific topic. For example, if students are creating a project about the Great Depression, the teacher can compile a folder with images pulled from the Library of

Congress. Then, it's just a matter of recording voiceovers and choosing images that agree with each line of the script.

Another strategy to fit moviemaking into your curriculum is to help students produce movie projects to showcase what they have learned from their Genius Hour projects. Many teachers implement Genius Hour, sometimes called 20% Time. During this hour each week, students are allowed to self-select a topic for research or exploration. Students can even choose to undertake learning a new skill or perhaps devise a way to help their community. The point of Genius Hour is to provide students an opportunity to choose their learning and through doing so, develop as lifelong learners. It is incredibly empowering for students to make choices and find ways to share!

I have implemented Genius Hour in my own classroom. Students posed questions and each person selected one to answer. A few kids chose to work collaboratively, while others preferred to be independent. As we started seeking answers for our questions, some students leveraged YouTube, others explored websites, several contacted experts to interview, and a handful conducted experiments or created artwork. At the

Susan Diaz Cuevas, ELEMENTARY INSTRUCTIONAL COACH, FIRST-GRADE TEACHER

"In elementary classrooms, digital storytelling can be integrated during center time or small groups. While teaching an English Language Development class, my students would create movie projects to practice their language skills. They recorded voiceovers for our whole-class collaborative projects during designated ELD time. Students were given the chance to practice their speaking skills authentically. We also always took iPads with us when we went on field trips. Upon our return, students could share their learning using the original footage they had collected throughout the day. After school programs, enrichment clubs, recess—all of these are great opportunities to introduce digital storytelling. As student experts develop, they can assist teachers in moviemaking in the classroom setting—which saves tons of time."

end of our exploration phase, students created movies to showcase their learning. Some movie projects ended up being informational, while others were more about demonstrating a newly developed skill. All included a reflection component at the end, which was filmed as a vlog. Other teachers I have talked to have structured similar projects, in both elementary and secondary classes. Thus, Genius Hour can be a viable option for moviemaking integration at any age level or subject area.

In the end, every worthwhile endeavor in the classroom takes time. With purposeful lesson design and a flexible approach, moviemaking can fit into any schedule. Certainly, the creativity, academic rigor, and engaging nature of moviemaking makes it a valuable instructional strategy that is well worth the time invested.

Overcoming the Challenge of Technology

Another barrier that teachers consistently identify as a reason they do not engage in more digital storytelling with their students is inequitable access to technology. Having taught a myriad of pilot programs for my district, my classroom has evolved greatly over the years. Though I began with the 24/7 MacBook Program, I also piloted a Bring Your Own Device Program, a 2:1 iPad Program, and a 1:1 Chromebook Program. Through all of these technology initiatives, I learned that it is possible for students to create movies whether they are sharing a handful of devices or have individual access.

Workflow

If a classroom has less than a 1:1 ratio of devices to students, planning to use those devices can be challenging. It is important to establish a workflow. Determine how students will keep track of which device they are using and develop a naming convention for labeling work that is housed on shared accounts. For example, if a classroom is using several iPads, the teacher should know that iMovie projects are saved locally on each tablet, making it important for students to use the same device each time. Each of the students who use a particular iPad should include their first name and last initial in their project's title. By contrast, a classroom that uses Chromebooks and browser-based programs with cloud storage makes it possible for students to continue their work using any Chromebook. Clearly establish expectations about how to show respect for the work of others, and consider having students work together to brainstorm a list of behaviors to avoid, such as not opening a file that doesn't belong to you, as well as behaviors to promote, such as making sure to plug in a device when you're done using it.

With shared devices, time spent on the device should be used for filming or editing. All other planning work, such as brainstorming, scripting, or storyboarding, will likely occur offline. In that situation, it helps to have a mechanism for keeping track of student work and progress. Keeping student work on clipboards or in file folders that stay in the room is important. Doing so will help you avoid the dreaded "I left it at home" explanation. I have used clipboards in the past, because there is something about clipboards that middle school students seem to find official-feeling and fun. These clipboards were stored in plastic milk crates beneath each table group. Some secondary teachers might prefer that students store their work in folders, which can then be gathered and placed in a crate for each individual period.

Since students will need to access technology to film, collect images, record voice-overs, and edit, inverted learning models can again prove worthwhile. The station rotation blended model allows for online and offline stations, which makes it ideal. If storytelling is a priority in your instruction, then being flexible and inventive is crucial.

Leveraging Other Devices

If it is in keeping with your school's policy, you might consider allowing students to utilize their own personal devices for moviemaking. Some students may already be familiar with specific apps for video editing. Don't worry about whether you have familiarity with the program they intend to use. Simply remind students to make responsible use of their time and technology and let them worry about how to accomplish the task you've set forth. Some of the most creative moviemaking choices my students have were made possible because they were able to use their own devices. Universally, I have found that when a student uses their own phone or tablet, they tend to work on their project outside of school as well. This really encourages a sense of ownership and personal investment.

Equipment

All you really need to get started is a portable recording device of some kind and any type of video editing application. My students regularly record using the cameras built into their Chromebooks, but some also like to use their personal cell phones or tablets. There is a frequent misconception that moviemaking can only be accomplished using pricey cameras or the latest iPhone—not true! In digital storytelling, the primary emphasis should always be placed on the story itself. A great many technical inadequacies can be forgiven if only there is an excellent story at the heart of every student-created movie.

When filming on location with students who are producing a short film or a news segment, external microphones, tripods, boom equipment, reflectors, and other high-end tools can be useful and effective. However, over the years I have found that moviemaking in core content areas requires simplicity. If teachers have time to cover the proper use of such equipment and the funding to buy it, more power to them. However, when teachers work within the confines of curriculum and pacing guides, it is absolutely okay to not use all of the fancy gear. To be honest, I usually do not. Give yourself permission to keep it simple.

If your students are using Chromebooks, there are several browser-based video editors available. I tend to gravitate toward WeVideo, because my district has a subscription. However, there is a free version that students can use, too. Animoto is another example of a browser-based editor, as is Adobe Spark. Keep in mind that in order for students to use Adobe, they must be 13 years of age or older, so that tool is generally limited to secondary schools. If your students are using iPads, then iMovie is the standard option for video editing. It has a simple interface that is easy for even the youngest of students to understand. Animation apps, such as Powtoon or Toontastic, can make the storytelling process especially fun. In secondary classrooms, it is popular for students to request to use their cell phones and video editing apps they are already familiar with; in these instances, my response is usually "Go for it!" It is not necessary for teachers to be experts on any of these platforms. Simply point students in the direction of the tool and they will more than likely figure it out far better than we can.

Audio is the area where a little help goes a long way. Half of video is audio, and if viewers are unable to make sense of a voiceover, it compromises the integrity of the story. So, while there is a ton of mobile filmmaking equipment available, a pair of earbuds with a built-in microphone can exponentially improve the quality of student work. Earbuds are especially helpful when students are using Chromebooks or other devices with weak microphones. Loud, clear audio capture is essential in the storytelling process. Since most of the projects my students undertake involve recording a voiceover, this is my one must-have piece of technology that can be easily acquired at a dollar discount store.

Helping Students Tell Their Truth

During the course of my professional development classes, I share a wide variety of student-created movies that have emerged from my classroom over the years. Since many of the stories are poignant, thought-provoking, and transparent in their vulnerability, workshop participants inevitably ask, "How do you get them to write like that? To say those things? To share their truths?"

The reality is students cross the classroom threshold carrying a lot of baggage, most of which we cannot easily discern. For many of my students, middle school is the time to fit in and sometimes hide. Thus, getting them to open up is a process that takes continuous effort. Classroom culture is the key to unlocking student voices, which can then be lifted by fostering ongoing opportunities to speak up and speak out. It is necessary for adults to recognize that we do not know what it is to be a young person in today's world. Poverty, family problems, impossible beauty standards, cyberbullying, feeling "less than" compared to others—all of these issues and more directly impact our students. Building a positive classroom culture that values every individual, operates on respect, and forges trust—that is the type of environment capable of inspiring students to share their stories.

The Golden Share

One of the ways in which I encourage honest storytelling is by applying the Golden Rule to the process of sharing. When I want to encourage students to write about difficult things, to share pieces of themselves with each other, I lead the way by sharing my own stories. It is difficult to ask students to do tasks that we ourselves would not undertake, and children of all ages are able to recognize authenticity—or the lack of it—from a mile away. So, I instituted the Golden Share, which means that whenever we take on particularly deep movie projects, I always share my writing with students before asking them to share their writing with me. In addition to allowing us to connect on a human level, letting students read my scripts or watch drafts of my movies helps foster a creative culture and a bond of trust. It also allows me to model how to receive feedback from others, and how to respond productively.

A few years ago, as the spring film festival season approached, we prepared to write personal narratives. We revisited the idea of what makes compelling stories and rewatched some of our favorite movies made by previous students. We reviewed

Jamie O'Neil, HIGH SCHOOL JOURNALISM TEACHER

"Moviemaking is about seeing a special spark in each student. A lot of my high schoolers initially don't believe that they are storytellers, or they think that they can't be successful because writing isn't their forte. In truth, most don't even realize that they have a story to tell! So, I use prompts to get them thinking, to help them see their own potential. My message to students is that they matter, they are interesting, and they are special."

story structure and the importance of moments of revelation, and then I shared my personal narrative script. I wrote about my mom, what it was like to lose her a few months prior, and how one of the most difficult aspects of grief is all of the unanswered questions left behind. I had a lifetime of questions that I didn't even know I wanted answers to, and no one to whom I could ask them. Students read my script quietly. Afterward, one girl, who had a particularly tough exterior and did not often speak unless her words were loaded with sarcasm, raised her hand. "Mrs. Pack, I get you. That's really sad and I can relate, you know? Thanks for sharing that with us."

Whether reading my script acted as a catalyst or she simply reached a point of readiness, this student ended up writing a personal narrative about her dad and how he had disappeared a few years before. She wrote about how her mother worried that her father had died somewhere in Mexico, while her older brother wondered if maybe he had another family somewhere. She didn't know what to think and concluded her script by musing about what it would be like to see him again. Even though this student did not finish creating her entire movie project, she did finish the script and about two-thirds of the edit, which was more work than she had completed during the course of the entire trimester. I felt honored that she chose to share such a personal story, and grateful that she felt comfortable enough to do so.

Community Building

Teachers tend to be excellent community builders. Most of the educators I have met over the years are very conscious of the effect that a strong sense of community can have on their classrooms. It can come as no surprise that the best storytelling occurs when students feel intensely connected to one another. In order to ensure this type of connectivity, storytelling must be woven into the social fabric of the room.

So much of the storytelling process is collaborative: brainstorming, group script writing, giving and receiving feedback, troubleshooting technology, crowd-sourcing editing techniques, celebrating and critiquing finished products. Each of the activities cannot occur in isolation. As teachers, we need to model how to fully and properly engage in these processes. Part of creative freedom comes from knowing there is no single accepted answer. Some of the students who struggle with storytelling tend to be those for whom open-ended tasks are disconcerting. They are used to having only one correct answer, and that is the antithesis of every creative task. Educators must praise divergent thinking, the strategic use of tools, and student expertise. This practice shifts the power dynamic from teacher-centered to student-centered and makes creative risk-taking desirable.

There is value in whole-group feedback. I will often share a rough cut of a digital story I am working on and model how to ask others for feedback. Students need to see that it is okay to receive constructive comments, and what it looks like when one does so productively. When they offer input and I do not respond defensively, but rather with a "tell me more" attitude, it takes away any potential sting of criticism and puts the focus on the story. Whole group feedback may not be comfortable for every student, so I typically ask for one or two volunteers who would like to share with the whole group, then break the rest of the feedback session into smaller groups. Remind students that they ultimately retain creative control, and that whether or not they choose to act on points of feedback is entirely up to them.

The Importance of Tearing Down Barriers

The twin barriers of time and technology can be challenging, and getting students to share their truth is no easy task. However, breaking down these barriers is essential. Students are hungry for expression and genuinely in need of a storytelling outlet to foster their creativity and cultivate their voices. Pacing guides can be managed, even limited resources can be leveraged, and classroom communities can be built one brick of trust at a time. No matter where you are in your journey as a storytelling teacher, validate what you have accomplished for your students so far, and then push yourself to do more. Prioritize storytelling in your curriculum, take steps to plan efficient and effective implementation, and do not be afraid to think outside the box. Continue to advocate for what your students need most—more opportunities to tell the stories of their learning, their lives, and their futures.

Part 3

Getting Started with Students

Chapter 8

Quick-Start Moviemaking Lesson Ideas

The integration of moviemaking is often addressed from a bird's-eye view, more theoretical than practical. The purpose of this chapter is to provide you with some quick-start lesson plans that require minimal preparation to execute. They are impactful, capable of building emotional resonance, and concrete. If you are a new storytelling teacher, then you may be eager to begin but feel overwhelmed by the possibilities. If you are a veteran storytelling teacher, you might be looking for some fresh ideas. In either case, the following lesson frames are flexible and can be applied to any content area or grade level. For your convenience, each lesson is also connected to ISTE standards, which are explicitly outlined. Templates and resources are included at the end of this chapter, and my hope is that you will find each lesson easy to implement with positive student results. All of these lessons have been used in both my classroom and others, so please know that they are teacher-approved!

The "I Am" Poem

Teachers generally use "I Am" poems to get to know their students; as a brand-new teacher, I certainly did. This type of poem follows a specific structure meant to explore a person's perception of the world and themselves. In order to write an "I Am" poem, students first identify who they are, then fill in a variety of statements about what they see, smell, taste, feel, fear, dream, etc. As an interpersonal tool, writing these poems can build community. However, it is even more powerful as an academic tool. Typically, for the first moviemaking project of the year, I ask students to write and create a movie to bring their personal "I Am" poem to life. The following iterations of "I Am" poems focus on characters in the texts we read, historical figures, collectives, literary devices, or significant objects and ideas pertaining to content. In science and math, "I Am" poems can be used to personify concepts such as cellular mitosis, gene therapy, organic farming, rational numbers, the order of operations, and more. With each repetition of this poetry format, students become more adept at the storytelling process—especially the writing and editing components.

The advantage of the "I Am" poem format is that it storifies information that might otherwise be delivered as a report or strictly informational text. This allows emotional beats to emerge and the content to become more engaging. Emotional resonance activates student learning, which then becomes sticky. One of the teachers I worked with through professional development opted to teach fourth-grade standards pertaining to Native American history using an "I Am" poem. Students researched various tribes using multiple sources, wrote poems from the point of view of an imagined individual in each tribe, and then selected appropriate images to authentically represent each tribe's culture. With such a project, the teacher had two different metrics by which to evaluate each student's understanding of content: the script the student wrote and the visuals they chose to communicate their learning. The degree to which students were able to practice effective research and information literacy skills also made this project a vastly superior alternative to the one the teacher had traditionally implemented. Ongoing growth in terms

WATCH SAMPLE "I AM" POEM PROJECTS

of the way we teach history, science, and language centers on the analysis of multiple perspectives. What better way to allow students to examine people, places, and ideas than through a digital story such as this?

ISTE Standards:

- ✦ Empowered Student (1a, 1c)
- ✦ Knowledge Constructor (3a-c)
- ✦ Digital Citizen (2c)
- ✦ Creative Communicator (6a-d)

Instructional Sequence: Introduce the storytelling task at the beginning of a unit of study for your content area. Engage in whatever instruction you normally would, peppering in the audiovisual literacy mini lessons as needed.

- ✦ **Introduction:** Once you reach the culmination of the unit, provide students with the "I Am" poem template and rubric. Consider watching an anchor video if it is the first content-based poem your students have ever created as a movie. Abbreviate the template as needed for students who require additional language support or accommodations.

- ✦ **Script Writing:** Structure the writing process as appropriate for your students. With the first iteration of an "I Am" poem, it can be helpful to make scripting a collaborative process. I have used group writing with honors classes, students on par with grade-level expectations, struggling students, English learners, and students with special needs. For all of these groups, cooperative scripting can be a dynamic and engaging way to synthesize content; it also reduces some of the cognitive load while promoting organic language practice. With subsequent iterations of the "I Am" poem project, students will be more comfortable writing on an individual basis—and that is the ultimate goal. The writing is a direct reflection of their learning, so as a summative performance assessment, it makes sense that student work would eventually become independent.

- ✦ **Feedback:** Choose a feedback mechanism that is appropriate for your educational context. It is important to provide feedback on scripts before allowing students to proceed. This helps to catch and correct errors before the project is finished; feedback is an opportunity to provide "just in time" support and validate student understanding. Because feedback is necessary, this is another good rationale for collaborative writing. Reviewing seven or eight scripts is definitely easier than checking 35. Throughout the feedback process, ensure that students understand how to read the rubric and ask them to reference it if they are providing peer feedback.

✦ **Audiovisual Planning:** Have students create storyboards or two-column scripts to notate preferred visuals for their project. This will provide direction when students begin to collect audio and visual assets to make their movie.

✦ **Asset Collection:** In any project that is reliant on a voiceover, students should first record themselves reading their script. Remember to provide an opportunity for practice before asking students to record and help clarify pronunciation. After voices have been recorded, students should locate images and access any stock media libraries contained in their video editing programs or apps. Remind students to properly filter their web searches for images that are free to use and share. Also, reinforce that proper citation is a necessity.

✦ **Editing:** Reiterate the concept of agreement, and prompt students to edit using whichever tools are at their disposal. Since students record their voice-overs as the first step in asset collection, the editing process will move much faster. Students should be able to listen to their voice recording using earbuds and match relevant images or video to what they are saying. If students have not previously been instructed about the Ken Burns effect, this would be a good time to teach that mini lesson. If they have received instruction about this type of push-and-pull animation, then simply remind them about the tool. Music, sound effects, credits, transitions, and other effects can be layered in at any point after the arrangement of voiceover and visuals. It is helpful to stop several times throughout this process and ask students to review the rubric.

✦ **Publishing:** Celebrate student work by hosting a class viewing party, uploading to a learning management system, or sharing in small groups. The Glows and Grows protocol (see chapter 4) works well for providing feedback that is

both affirming and growth-oriented, so that the next iteration of content-based "I Am" poems is even better.

Resources:

✦ "I Am" poem template

✦ "I Am" poem rubric

The "In My Time" Project

One of my favorite ways to include storytelling in a manner that amplifies under-represented voices and perspectives is the "In My Time" project. This project is an opportunity for students to examine subject matter through the dual lenses of a specific individual and the historical context of their life. While reading an excerpt from *Warriors Don't Cry* by Melba Patillo Beals, one of the first Black students to integrate Little Rock Central High School, my students examined other significant figures in Black history. After reading the autobiographical novel *The Circuit* by Francisco Jimenez, a migrant farm laborer, students studied the life of Cesar Chavez, a Mexican American activist who established the United Farm Workers Movement during the 1960s. For both of these units of study, my students used a template to write about who an important individual was, what they accomplished, and what they hoped for the future. All of this was framed by the context in which they lived, so the "In My Time" template asks students to reflect on the cultural norms of the time.

STEM integrations are also possible for this project. One math teacher I worked with had her students create an "In My Time" project about female mathematicians, while a science teacher who took one of my classes decided to ask his students to create movies about Neil deGrasse Tyson, a Black astrophysicist. With a universal template, this project allows students to amplify the contributions of people of color and other underrepresented populations, making equity a centerpiece of both classroom culture and instruction.

ISTE Standards:

✦ Digital Citizen (2c)   ✦ Creative Communicator (6a-d)

✦ Knowledge Constructor (3a-c)

Instructional Sequence: Introduce the storytelling task at the beginning of the instructional unit. Emphasize that the goal of this project is to promote equity and inclusion pertaining to the study of your subject area.

✦ **Introduction:** Ask students to research the contributions of historical or contemporary figures using multiple sources. If teachers are implementing this project for the specific purpose of honoring Black History Month, consider using *The Undefeated 44* website, which features contributions of Black Americans in a variety of fields, as referenced in chapter 3.

✦ **Script Writing and Audiovisual Planning:** Provide students with the "In My Time" template and discuss each of the three sections. The first stanza provides historical context, the second stanza showcases a person's achievements, and the third stanza examines the lasting cultural and/or academic impact that defines the person's legacy. Help students understand that these three stanzas exemplify the emotional beats of a good story: an inciting condition or incident, the development of tension, and the triumph of the human spirit. This can be a collaborative or individual task. Typically, my students create this movie project after they have made several movies based on other templates, so they are comfortable writing scripts. For that reason, this is usually an individual project in my classroom. However, remember to make choices that work for you, your students, and your content area. There is no right or wrong way to structure the writing process here. After scripting, have students prepare storyboards or two-column notes to identify the visual components that will accompany their voiceover script.

✦ **Feedback:** Peer feedback in small groups is a strong option for this project, because it not only assists in project development, but also gives students the opportunity to learn about as many people as possible. The conversations that emerge during this feedback round are impactful and worthwhile. Peer review is meant to refine the script as much as it is to solidify the types of images or video clips students will need to locate, so make sure that storyboards or two-column notes are well-prepared ahead of time.

✦ **Asset Collection:** This project relies on a voiceover, so students must record their scripts first, either in class or at home. Collecting images will be challenging to varying degrees, largely dependent on the time period the person was alive as well as historical bias against people of color, queer people, etc. The Library of Congress can be a useful resource for students to leverage when looking for images that exemplify the historical context of the day. Make sure you discuss and clarify students' understanding as needed. For example, one of my students researched Sojourner Truth, a formerly enslaved person who escaped and became an outspoken advocate for abolition. In the first stanza of the student's project, he wrote the words, "In my time, slavery was an injustice faced in silence." Another student, who researched Dr. Charles R. Drew, also mentioned slavery in the contextual portion of the template. However, Dr. Drew was born in the twentieth century. As the first African American to earn a doctorate from Columbia University, he became the world's leading authority on blood transfusions. While he experienced discrimination in the lead-up to the Civil Rights Movement, he was never enslaved, so the line the student provided for historical context was not the most directly relevant. This error was not caught in the feedback process because my sixth-grade students have a more limited understanding of the scope of American history. Therefore, it is essential for teachers to continue to monitor historical accuracy and offer course correction as needed. There will inevitably be certain time periods and issues that require clarification from an adult as students search for images. This is also a time to reinforce the concepts of fair use and proper citation.

✦ **Editing:** Since the script is already recorded as a voiceover, students can focus the majority of their time on matching their images to their audio. A clear understanding of agreement and how to appropriately use the Ken Burns effect is necessary for projects like this one that mainly comprise photos. Finding appropriate music tracks may prove challenging, as many of the music tracks preloaded in editing programs like iMovie are more upbeat and contemporary in nature. Emphasize that music does not necessarily have to be authentic to the time, but rather appropriate for the mood and tone of the movie. Most of the "In My Time" projects my students have created ended up with soft, serious instrumental tracks, which makes sense given the solemn subject matter often embedded in the historical context of their stories. To save time, you could compile a folder of copyright-free music before students reach this stage.

✦ **Publishing:** The goal of this project is to amplify the achievements of marginalized populations. Make sure to celebrate student work and the under-represented people that were researched. If privacy policies allow, upload movie projects to YouTube, share on school social media accounts, or make movies shareable to circulate at your school.

Resources:

✦ "In My Time" template

✦ "In My Time" rubric

The 15-Second Story

The concept of economy of detail is difficult for students to grasp. Students also have a tendency to write scripts that are too large in scope or include excessive detail that distracts from the story they are telling. This issue is compounded by an almost universal instinct among new video editors to let clips or images run longer than necessary. One of my favorite ways to foster brevity, precision editing skills, and film angle fluency is the 15-Second Story.

This type of movie project can function as either a check for understanding or a summative assessment to conclude a smaller lesson arc. It can also work well as a method of storytelling to learn, one of the two moviemaking integration paths discussed in chapter 5. Teachers should be aware that the film angle mini lesson is a prerequisite, as 15-Second Stories rely on original video footage filmed by students. This type of project is collaborative by nature and most effective in groups of three. Students begin by brainstorming the facts, ideas, or concepts most integral to the content they have just learned. Then, students storify the content, which can be challenging considering the amount of time allowed for the finished product—only 15 seconds, not including title or credits. Teachers can use this project to have students summarize content, retell a narrative, or extrapolate main ideas. A high school math teacher in my district had her students create 15-Second Stories about polynomial functions, while a science teacher focused on the water cycle. In my classroom, I've had students showcase the achievements of Alexander the Great, illuminate the benefits of irrigation, and illustrate the concept of suspense.

The short nature of the finished product curtails the amount of time needed for students to write, storyboard, and film. Surprisingly, the most involved stage of the storytelling process for this project is editing. Inevitably, students will find that even their brief scripts are too long, forcing them to reevaluate their writing, pare back ideas, rearrange components, and problem-solve ways to communicate other than dialogue. While editing, students quickly discover that even half a second makes a difference as they trim each clip with precision in order to meet the 15-second time limit. This storytelling project, though short, carries a significant cognitive load, which is why collaboration is key.

ISTE Standards:

✦ Knowledge Constructor (3a-c)

✦ Creative Communicator (6a-d)

Instructional Sequence: Preview the storytelling task at the outset of instruction; as students process the subject matter content, they should already be thinking about which pieces of information are most important to embed in their scripts.

✦ **Introduction:** Remind students about the film angles they have learned. Consider assigning a film angle sorting activity as review or use an online game interface such as Kahoot! or Quizizz to activate students' prior knowledge. Explain to students that the 15-second time limit will be rigidly enforced because one of the goals is to practice concise but impactful storytelling.

✦ **Script Writing:** Due to the collaborative nature of this project, script writing should occur in groups of no more than three. Students will utilize their collective knowledge to write content-based stories that are compelling. Reiterate that stories are compelling when they build emotional tension. This doesn't necessarily mean that effective stories are serious; they can also be humorous, scary, or joyful. Finding an appropriate mood or tone to establish is a key part of the scripting process for this project. Once students have identified their approach, it only takes about 15–20 minutes to script. If needed, show students a 15-second clip of a movie or trailer in order to drive home how little time they have to communicate their ideas. Scripts and visual planning can be easily combined using a storyboard, which also accelerates the time it takes for students to execute preproduction.

✦ **Feedback:** This stage of the storytelling process is indispensable because it will help students gauge the clarity of their writing. Pitch groups are an excellent mechanism for feedback. Pair two groups together and let them pitch their script to one another using the procedures outlined in chapter 4. It will quickly become apparent if important information is lacking, and seeing how others have executed the same task is an opportunity for growth. Students can help one another problem-solve how content can be relayed nonverbally through the use of certain images, props, or music. Some of my students have even brought homemade costumes to use based on suggestions made in their pitch groups.

✦ **Asset Collection:** Recording original footage can be time-consuming, so make certain students have established a list of shots they need to collect before they are allowed to begin filming. It is important to establish a hard time limit for filming to provide impetus for efficiency. The time management skills built during the course of this project will manifest during subsequent projects. Students often need to leave the classroom and move around campus in order to film. I like to provide a stopwatch to each group because asking middle school students to keep an eye on the clock does not hold up during the excitement of recording. We thoroughly discuss how to be considerate of other groups who are filming, other classrooms full of students learning, and any adults they may encounter. Campus security has become used to seeing my students film outside of our classroom; in fact, everyone on campus seems to recognize room 208 kids as they are out and about quite often. Providing advance notice to administration or other pertinent staff members is a courtesy that should not be overlooked.

✦ **Editing:** Video footage should be uploaded to a shared Google Drive folder so it is accessible to the entire group. Students can either edit collaboratively (depending on availability of devices) or each student can make their own individual cut. There are advantages to both strategies: Creating one edit using a single computer fosters discussion and creative thinking; however, if the student whose account has been used for editing is absent, then a group may become unable to work or be forced to start over. This concern is rendered moot if students are using classroom devices that do not require users to sign in to individual accounts. Another strategy is asking each student to edit their own cut, which effectively ensures that all students remain engaged in the creation process. On the other hand, it tends to discourage collaborative conversations as each student becomes immersed in their own work. Choose an editing strategy that best works for your students, grade level, and content area.

✦ **Publishing:** The 15-Second Story project lends itself well to a classroom show-case. Since each product is short, teachers might consider showing each group's work. Provide an opportunity for Glows and Grows after each movie is shown. This can typically be accomplished in one class period or less.

Resources:

✦ 15-Second Story task sheet

✦ 15-Second Story rubric

The Acrostic Poem

Poetry is obviously one of my favorite mechanisms for storytelling in core content areas. Acrostic poems utilize a single word to provide structure; the word is written vertically and each letter in the word begins a line. Each line typically reveals more information and details about a topic. Taken as a whole, the lines communicate a uniform message that conveys content-area knowledge. By sixth grade, many of my students have prior experience reading or writing acrostics. However, a teacher of younger grades might need to frontload more in-depth regarding how this type of poetry works. Elementary students might even benefit from writing an acrostic poem using their names before attempting a poem based on subject matter.

Acrostics are easily integrated into any curriculum because word choice is entirely flexible. This moviemaking project can be used with varying complexity, ranging from a simple way for students to acquire domain-specific vocabulary to an in-depth analysis of a particular topic.

ISTE Standards:

✦ Empowered Student (1a, 1c)

✦ Digital Citizen (2c)

✦ Knowledge Constructor (3a-c)

✦ Creative Communicator (6a-d)

Instructional Sequence: Preview the storytelling task at the outset of the unit and revisit it throughout. This provides students with a greater context for their learning. Make it clear that the endgame is not the graphic organizers, open-ended questions, or other academic tasks they might undertake during the course of a unit. Rather, the endgame is the story they will tell to express their mastery of content.

✦ **Introduction:** Teachers can use acrostics as a means to learn or as summative assessments. Regardless of the pathway you choose for integration, you will have to ensure that students are familiar with the structure of acrostic poems. Whether you choose to provide a few minutes for students to search Google for examples or carefully curate a few of your own, it is important for students to read mentor texts to anchor their understanding.

✦ **Script Writing:** The first step in the writing process is word selection. Students can either utilize the same word or choose from a selection provided by the teacher. Words should directly relate to content. Before writing lines, ask students to brainstorm important information that should be included somehow in the acrostic. Brainstorming should be a collaborative task, providing an opportunity to sort ideas by level of importance. As students begin to draft their poems, some will struggle with repetitiveness. This is typically due to having exhausted all of their ideas, so teachers should be prepared to come alongside students who need extra support. A few well-placed guiding questions can easily get students back on track. Before seeking feedback, ask students to plan their visual components using a storyboard or two-column script.

✦ **Feedback:** This stage of the storytelling process is essential for fact-checking purposes. Ask students to share their acrostics in small groups. The following questions should guide student feedback: *Is the poem focused and informative? Do any of the ideas repeat? Where can word choice be refined? Are there emotional beats—problem, tension, solution?* Review what it is to be a critical friend, as opposed to offering critical cop-outs. The goal of feedback is improvement; reiterate this to students as often as necessary.

✦ **Asset Collection:** This type of project can utilize video clips, images, or a mixture of both. The concept of agreement is instrumental, so make sure students have a solid understanding about how audio and visual components must complement one another. As always, record the voiceover first and then begin the work of seeking visuals to bring the story to life. As a general rule of thumb, the visual should change as each line of the poem is read. Include frequent reminders for students to filter their image searches for resources that are free to use and share.

+ **Editing:** During the editing stage of the moviemaking process, teach students to exercise precision editing. As each line of the acrostic comes to an end, so should the image or video clip. Students have a tendency to let visuals run a second or two longer than necessary. As the voiceover moves on to the next line of the poem, the visual should change. This is the reason why it is so helpful to ensure students have recorded their voiceovers *before* they begin to edit. Often, errors in agreement occur when students transpose the process, editing images before recording their audio. This type of decision makes the editing process more complicated and can extend the amount of time students need to finish their projects. Efficiency is vital to giving students more opportunities to tell stories. As a teacher, insist that your students function as efficiently as possible.

+ **Publishing:** Validate student work by celebrating students' movies. Whether you choose to host a classroom viewing party, publish to a video-sharing site, or post work on social media, it is important for students to create for authentic audiences. If watching videos in class, consider using a small group SCALE activity to provide feedback. Every opportunity for celebration and feedback reinforces strong storytelling habits and identifies areas for future improvement.

Resources:

+ Acrostic Poem template
+ Acrostic Poem rubric

The Story Spine Project

As discussed throughout this book, storytelling that resonates has a three-act structure consisting of content that strikes emotional chords. Using a story spine helps students format their stories for maximum impact; it is a building block of the writing process and an effective jumping-off point for beginning storytellers. This project is useful in all content areas as students identify a character from whose point of view the subject matter can be conveyed. For example, when learning about the causes of World War I, a student could develop a character and storyline to explore the tension created by the assassination of Archduke Franz Ferdinand, Serbian nationalism, and conflicts over political alliances. In science, students could identify a person who experiences a problem that can be solved through scientific discovery or the use of scientific principles. In this case, the story becomes powerful as viewers experience empathy. In an English class, students can craft a narrative from the point of view of a forbidden book in the novel *Fahrenheit 451* by Ray Bradbury. In all of these subjects, the use of a story spine helps students tell their story in a way that establishes conflict, builds tension, and allows for a moment of realization or triumph.

When teachers ask students to write a story without providing any structure, the results are mixed. Some students include too much detail, while others do not include enough. Sometimes students have trouble staying focused or relaying events in an order that makes sense. Story spines eliminate the bulk of these issues while fostering engaging storytelling habits.

ISTE Standards:

+ Empowered Student (1a, 1c)
+ Knowledge Constructor (3a-c)
+ Digital Citizen (2c)
+ Creative Communicator (6a-d)

Instructional Sequence: Story Spine projects are deceptively easy. However, the implementation of this project takes careful planning and support, particularly during the scripting process. Collaborative writing might be a good strategy to employ, particularly if students are relatively inexperienced storytellers.

✦ **Introduction:** As always, preview the storytelling task at the start of a unit. This extends the amount of time students have to think about the type of story it could be possible to tell.

✦ **Script Writing:** Providing an anchor text is essential for this project. Teachers should draft a similar but unrelated sample script to show students how subject matter can be embedded in a story. One of the first challenges students will face is how to develop a character. Encourage them to select someone who has a personal stake in the story being told. Examples might include a witness to a historical event, a community member seeking a solution, or a person who stands to gain or lose something by the end of the story. Significant items can also function as creative narrators. One of my students once told a story about a bolt of silk fabric traveling along the Silk Road during the Han dynasty. Other perspectives that could have worked just as well include a silk merchant, a child living in a trading post, or a sailor loading the silk onto a ship bound for the Roman Empire by way of the Mediterranean Sea. Once students select a point of view, they must then decide on the setting, action, and resolution. The Story Spine template functions as a basic skeleton; students can add more lines as needed.

✦ **Feedback:** For this type of project, I typically like to provide feedback to each of my students rather than relying on peer feedback mechanisms. Since the Story Spine project conveys content through a narrative, it is helpful for students to know whether they have embedded enough subject matter knowledge in their actual story. This is a level of feedback best provided by the teacher. I read scripts and provide feedback using the teacher-led station during blended instruction. However, several of my colleagues simply ask their students to write scripts, then take anywhere from a few days to a week to provide feedback via voice comments in Google Docs. (My favorite extension for voice comments is Mote, which is available on the Chrome Web Store.)

✦ **Asset Collection:** Filming live footage for this type of project can be time-consuming and may be nearly impossible for some topics. For this reason, I generally

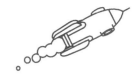

recommend that teachers have students collect still images and apply the Ken Burns effect wisely. As previously mentioned in this chapter, if students have access to stock media libraries within their editing software, asset collection will move even more quickly. Since the Story Spine project relies on a voiceover, it is also best for students to record that first before worrying about visual components. Set clear digital citizenship expectations regarding the intellectual property of others. If needed, demonstrate how to use advanced search features to help students locate only images that are free to use and share.

✦ **Editing:** These digital stories should be approximately 1 1/2–2 minutes in length. As students create, they may find a need to pare back on their scripts. As long as the emotional integrity of the story is preserved, students may choose to convey certain details using visuals as opposed to audio statements. It helps to teach them how to split audio tracks so that they may cut out parts of their voiceovers as needed, which eliminates the need to rerecord audio. Visually, transitions communicate the passage of time, which may be integral to the stories that students are telling. Help students understand how signal words and transitions work together in the editing process. If a change of space or time is indicated by the script, then a cross-dissolve transition might be a visually literate choice. However, remind students that editing effects are like salt: a little bit goes a long way. Over-the-top transition patterns—such as mosaics, spinning blocks, or other flipping images—will likely take away from the story rather than add to it.

✦ **Publishing:** One of my favorite methods to share work on a classroom level is to ask students to watch and comment using the Round Table strategy. Each student at a table group loads their movie on their device, then students rotate clockwise from one seat to the next. While watching each movie, students record comments—two specific, positive points and one area for future improvement—on sticky notes that are left at each spot. Once students arrive back at their original seats, they read the comments and complete a reflection in order to process the feedback from their peers. This type of viewing party fosters metacognition and prepares students for future project iterations.

Resources:

- ✦ Story Spine template
- ✦ Story Spine rubric

**DOWNLOAD ALL
CHAPTER RESOURCES**

Chapter 9

Storytelling in Online Learning Environments

Though virtual schools exist everywhere, and online teachers are used to operating in 100% digital settings, many educators have only just begun to explore virtual learning. As veteran online instructors know, digital classroom culture must be purposefully cultivated; otherwise, students may feel disconnected and lonely on their academic journeys. One study published in the *Journal of the American Academy of Child and Adolescent Psychiatry* found that socially isolated children have a greater probability of mental health struggles (Matthews et al., 2015). So, helping students connect to one another—even at a distance—is essential for long-term health.

Shane Frakes, SEVENTH-GRADE TEACHER

"I'm always in pursuit of what is contemporary, and how I can infuse it into my curriculum. The big question is, how do we make learning relevant and engaging for our students? So, I'm constantly on the hunt for what my students are into and how I can possibly leverage it. TikTok is something kids love right now. Recently, as I was browsing my feed, I kept seeing all of these 'tell me without telling me' videos, where people would illustrate their point of view on a topic without outright stating it. The videos were hilarious and after watching a few, it dawned on me that it might be a really cool way to introduce the concept of author's perspective. So, I asked my students to create a 'tell me without telling me' challenge video to share their point of view about online learning. In their video, they had to show the viewer how they felt without saying whether they love it or hate it. The actions, dialogue, and visuals had to do the job of communicating their perspective. Some kids created using multiple film angles edited together in WeVideo, while others utilized a single, long camera shot. Either way, kids published their challenge videos on FlipGrid, then analyzed one another's work in small groups. Collaborative discussion then revolved around whether students were able to discern one another's viewpoints based solely on the evidence provided in the video. My students created their videos asynchronously, then collaborated on their analysis synchronously, which made valuable use of our live class time."

Moviemaking is one avenue that can lead to a greater sense of connectedness among students. Digital storytelling can occur in any instructional setting. Whether classrooms are fully online or formatted as blended or hybrid learning environments, students deserve the opportunity to tell their stories. The academic value of storytelling, combined with the social emotional benefits inherent in activities that allow students to share their perspectives, justifies the effort required to plan and implement moviemaking in online settings.

On the continuum of engagement, students are most actively engaged when they are investing in and driving their learning, which includes asking questions, valuing

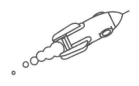

tasks, setting goals, seeking feedback, and self-assessing (Berry, 2020). In order for online teachers to fully engage their students, lessons must be high-interest and personally relevant. Students need to be able to not only find and use information, but also to create and share it. Fisher et al. (2020) stress the importance of asking students to share information because it encourages metacognition and fosters resilience. These authors specifically recommend a host of digital storytelling tools in order to accomplish this: WeVideo, Animoto, TikTok, and YouTube. When properly planned and executed, moviemaking can generate engagement and deep learning in the online environment.

The Quarantine Voices Project

In March 2020, schools in my Southern California county shut down due to the COVID-19 pandemic. At the time of the initial shutdown, my students had just fin-ished writing scripts for an individual narrative movie project. They were eager to see their stories come to life and many who had planned to shoot their own footage were disappointed when they realized that they would be unable to do so as a result of our state's order to shelter in place. Instead of shelving the idea of moviemaking, I decided to help my students regroup by reframing their projects into something more manageable for the type of education setting in which we found ourselves.

Schools shut down two weeks *before* our two-week spring break, so students spent a month on their own at home, adjusting to life during quarantine. I corresponded with many via email and social media and found that they were struggling to adapt. They were frightened of the unknown and wanted desperately to reconnect with their classmates. When instruction resumed via Google Meet, the storytelling assignment I posed was an acrostic project. Students were allowed to select any word as the subject of their acrostic poem, but during class discussion "quarantine" became the overwhelming word of choice. This type of project was more manage-able because there were only ten lines, which could easily become a voiceover. With students working at home among siblings, parents, and pets, there was a lot of potential for background noise. An overall lack of sustained privacy would surely affect the quality of a longer movie project, creating a potentially frustrating student experience. Since the acrostic audio component was a voiceover, students found it much easier to locate a quiet environment in which to record for 5-10 minutes. The scope of their prior projects simply didn't allow for that type of speed or adaptability.

Instructional Sequence

The Quarantine Voices project occurred in both my English Language Arts classes and my Associated Student Body government class. In both subjects, we close-read articles about coping with anxiety and educated ourselves about the coronavirus. We collaborated and deconstructed authors' arguments using graphic organizers, then made digital posters about ways to deal with stress. Students wrote drafts of their quarantine acrostics and provided feedback to one another during synchronous small group instruction. For students who could only participate asynchronously, feedback occurred in a Google Classroom discussion thread. We created simple two-column scripts to plan the audio and visual components and students were asked to seek out more feedback, either from family members or peers. They documented the feedback they received and their resulting editing choices using a Google Doc reflection form. In this way, much of the storytelling culture of our physical classroom was preserved, despite the virtual setting.

Student Results and Reaction

Students were extremely proud of their work. I started watching finished movies as soon as they began to trickle into our Google Classroom, and was struck by the way students talked about their stories. In a private comment one student said, "I really needed a project like this. Talking with other kids in class helped a lot. Our movies show where we're at in life right now which is cool."

QUARANTINE VOICES PLAYLIST

You can view some of the stories from Quarantine Voices using this QR code.

Considerations for Storytelling in Online Settings

As of the writing of this book, all public instruction in my district has been fully online for nearly a year. During that time, I have learned a lot about how to structure digital storytelling for success in online environments. One of the most important things to remember is that visual and audio literacies are cornerstones of digital storytelling. As tempting as it might be to pare back on the mini lessons, consider flipping them instead. Shifting instruction regarding film angles, agreement, audio literacy, and the Ken Burns effect into asynchronous space is a smart choice. Record a screencast, edit your own video, or find YouTube resources. I like to use Edpuzzle as the interface for my asynchronous mini lessons, because there is a built-in accountability component. Questions can be inserted into the video at certain time stamps and the video will automatically pause in order to allow students to answer. Make time to teach the SCALE mini lesson synchronously if possible and repeat it several times using various student examples. When students become used to critically viewing the work of others, they will begin creating their own from a more informed place.

When selecting moviemaking tasks, ensure that the scope of each project is manageable given any constraints your students may experience. Remember that repeated attempts at learning make all the difference in the world with regard to building storytelling fluency. Begin by building positive online classroom culture by having students create personal acrostic poems, "I Am" poems, or BioPoems. Then, shift to content-based storytelling using the same format as the personal project. This process repetition will generate creative confidence. The other advantage of these types of projects is that the writing process is naturally scaffolded. Students who require even more support can be accommodated during office hours or small group instruction.

As formative assessments, haiku projects are simple and easily accomplished in 20 minutes or less. Haiku has become one of my go-to projects for instruction in the online environment. After moving through a given lesson sequence, the independent practice task is to write a haiku poem that expresses the main idea of the content. Haiku consist of three lines. The first and third lines comprise five syllables each, while the second line is limited to seven. This 5-7-5 pattern is easily utilized by students of all ages. The brevity of the poem template ensures that students practice economy of detail. The images students choose to utilize enhance their message and provide visual information that might not have been able to fit into the haiku itself. This year I asked students to write haiku to describe the structure and importance of irrigation systems in the ancient world; they also wrote haiku to describe characters in the novel *The Tiger Rising* by Kate DiCamillo. Most recently, we created argumentative haiku on the topic of binge-watching after reading and researching using multiple sources. You can view examples of each of these haiku projects using the QR code provided.

WATCH STUDENT SAMPLES OF HAIKU

One of my favorite aspects of moviemaking in an online environment is the culture of helpfulness that emerges among students. Generally, I provide at least some

Stephanie Bronson, HIGH SCHOOL ENGLISH LANGUAGE DEVELOPMENT TEACHER

"One of my students is currently learning from her home in Mexico. She attends every single online class session and has never missed a day. For our latest moviemaking project, she enlisted the help of her entire family to film original footage using a phone. The assignment was to examine the issue of drug testing in schools, so students researched the topic and then wrote an 'I Am' poem from the point of view of a random drug tester. In her movie script, there is a line about how testing is expensive. My student exercised her agreement skills by filming her dad opening his wallet and handing out money. In another clip, her family acted out a conflict in the middle of their living room. This project brought them all together and the result was fantastic."

128

time to edit together during synchronous instruction; this usually occurs right at the beginning of the editing stage. Students are their own best resource, and they love to help one another. It also feels good to show what you know when a friend needs help troubleshooting. Though not strictly necessary, I find that beginning the editing process in a cooperative environment generates excitement and interaction among some of my quietest students. The remainder of the editing process can then be shifted into the asynchronous space.

Feedback is even more important in online learning environments, because there are not as many openings for casual conversation. It is essential to create opportunities for students to dialogue about their work, see the work of others, and think about creative choices. The peer review process can be easily shifted to asynchronous space. In order for students to access one another's videos, create shared folders with "anyone can edit" access. If you use Google Classroom, create an assignment where students attach a first draft. Then, post the link to the assignment folder that is located in *your* Google Drive. Adjust the folder permissions to "anyone can view."

If possible, I recommend providing at least some time for live discussion. SCALE can provide a framework to keep students focused (chapter 6), or you can limit discussion to one or two guiding questions if pressed for time. Remember that the most important questions for students to consider pertain to the element of story. Here are a few suggestions:

1. Does this story have emotional beats that resonate?

2. Is the message clearly communicated, or does anything interfere?

3. How does this story connect to what we are learning?

Celebrating student voices is crucial in online teaching and learning. The sense of community that develops as a result of celebration grows exponentially with each new story. It can be fun to have a watch party on Zoom or Google Meet, or you could make it a habit to show one or two student products at the end of each synchronous class. You can even start a discussion thread in your learning management system. Students can comment with the shareable link to their movie and reply to one another by offering specific feedback—Glows and Grows can be implemented even from a distance. I also like to share student videos using an "OurFlix" template that I developed as a nod to the Netflix experience. Students upload their videos to Google Drive or YouTube, and then screen capture a still frame image from their movie. We place those still frames on the tem-plate to mimic the movie thumbnails people are used to seeing

DOWNLOAD OURFLIX TEMPLATE

when they browse Netflix. Then, each thumbnail is linked to the video that each student created. OurFlix provides a fun and engaging way to curate and showcase student work within Google Classroom. It can even be shared on social media with the world at large, depending on your district's privacy policy. (See QR code 9.3.) No matter how we choose to do it, student voices need to be honored and celebrated. Knowing that others are listening can make young hearts soar and it can also create lifelong storytellers.

Acknowledgments

DIGICOM Learning has been instrumental in my growth as a teacher-storyteller. I will be forever grateful to the founders of DIGICOM: David Vogel, Larry Fulton, and Dr. Lee Grafton. Your faith in student voices transformed what learning looks like in classrooms across Southern California. Thank you for allowing me to be a part of the team. Many thanks also belong to Frank Guttler, Max Finneran, Maria Gitto, and all of the other film industry professionals, teacher-consultants, classroom specialists, artists in residence, and storytelling interns who contributed to the success of DIGICOM. I am especially indebted to David for allowing me to share the SCALE acronym developed by the curriculum integration team.

Many teachers contributed their wisdom during the writing of this book. I am overwhelmed with gratitude for these colleagues, whose classrooms reflect the power of digital storytelling: Lynn Yada, Julie Barda, Jamie O'Neil, Valcine Brown, Norman McKee, Mario Cruz, Sherry DiBari, Susan Diaz Cuevas, Virginia Gamboa, Stephanie Bronson, Shane Frakes, Dr. Lee Grafton, Frank Guttler, Ricardo Flores, and Brandon Pack.

Extra special thanks to my partner in crime, Georgia Terlaje. Your creative partnership has been an absolute joy! From DIGICOM, to our podcast, to webinars, and our many national conference presentations together—your expertise and friendship is priceless.

Sometimes digital storytelling looks a lot like organized chaos. I have been fortunate to have been enthusiastically supported by my district and school administrators over the years, most especially Greta Salmi and Brad Sauer. Thank you for opening doors, saying "yes," and fostering professional growth.

Finally, I am grateful to the students whose work appears in this book. Sincerest thanks to Marina, Gina, Nayef, Samantha, Niki, and Aubrie for sharing their personal stories. Gratitude goes to Bella, Dhaelene, Ava, Matthew, and Olivia for their

ACKNOWLEDGMENTS

Quarantine Voices Projects. Finally, thank you to Jazmin, AJ, Shareena, Karylle, and Katherine for their I Am Projects and haiku. To all of the students who are not named, thank you for your lessons and your voices.

References

American Film Institute. (2009). *Clint Eastwood: What makes a good Western* [Video]. YouTube. **https://youtu.be/-B8T6UJlkGc**

Andrews, E. (2015, December 18). *What is the oldest known piece of literature?* History. **https://www.history.com/news/what-is-the-oldest-known-piece-of-literature**

Berry, A. (2020). Disrupting to driving: Exploring upper primary teachers' perspectives on student engagement. *Teachers and Teaching, 26*(2), 145–165. **https://doi.org/10.1080/13540602.2020.1757421**

Brown, P. C., Roediger, H. L., & McDaniel, M. A. (2014). *Make it stick: The science of successful learning.* Belknap Press.

Coomes, P. (2011, November 15). *Daniel Meadows on digital literacy.* BBC News. **https://www.bbc.com/news/in-pictures-15717619**

Damasio, A. (2005). *Descartes' error: Emotion, reason and the human brain.* Penguin Books.

Ferrés, J., & Masanet, M. (2017). Communication efficiency in education: Increasing emotions and storytelling. [La eficacia comunicativa en la educación: Potenciando las emociones y el relato]. *Comunicar, 52,* 51–60. **https://doi.org/10.3916/C52-2017-05**

Fisher, D., Frey, N., & Hattie, J. (2021). *The distance learning playbook, grades K-12: Teaching for engagement and impact in any setting.* Corwin Press.

Gallo, C. (2019). Storytelling to inspire, educate, and engage. *American Journal of Health Promotion, 33*(3), 469–472. **https://doi.org/10.1177/0890117119825525b**

Groeneveld, E. (2017, February 12). *Chauvet Cave.* Ancient History Encyclopedia. **https://www.ancient.eu/Chauvet_Cave**

Hattie, J., & Timperley, H. (2007). The power of feedback. *Review of Educational Research, 77*(1), 81–112. **https://doi.org/10.3102/003465430298487**

REFERENCES

Hebern, M., & Corippo, J. (2018). *The EduProtocol field guide: 16 student-centered lesson frames for infinite learning possibilities*. Dave Burgess Consulting, Incorporated.

Hess, K. (2013). *A guide for using Webb's Depth of Knowledge with Common Core State Standards*. Common Core Institute. **https://education.ohio.gov/ getattachment/Topics/Teaching/Educator-Evaluation-System/How-to-Design-and-Select-Quality-Assessments/Webbs-DOK-Flip-Chart.pdf.aspx**

Hurley, R. (2017). *Making your teaching something special: 50 simple ways to become a better teacher*. Dave Burgess Consulting, Incorporated.

Khan Academy. *Story spine* [Video]. Khan Academy. **https://www.khanacademy. org/humanities/hass-storytelling/storytelling-pixar-in-a-box/ ah-piab-story-structure/v/video1a-fine**

Kurlaender, M., Reed, S., Cohen, K., Naven, M., Martorell, P., & Carrell, S. (2018, December). *Where California students attend college*. Policy Analysis for California Education. **https://edpolicyinca.org/publications/ where-california-high-school-students-attend-college**

Matthews, T., Danese, A., Wertz, J., Ambler, A., Kelly, M., Diver, A., Caspi, A., Moffitt, T. E., & Arseneault, L. (2015). Social isolation and mental health at primary and secondary school entry: A longitudinal cohort study. *Journal of the American Academy of Child & Adolescent Psychiatry*, 54(3), 225–232. **https://doi.org/10.1016/j.jaac.2014.12.008**

Meadows, D. *Digital storytelling*. Photobus. **http://www.photobus.co.uk/ digital-storytelling**

Muybridge, E. (1878). *The horse in motion. "Sallie Gardner," owned by Leland Stanford; running at a 1:40 gait over the Palo Alto track, 19th June 1878 / Muybridge* [Photograph]. The Library of Congress, United States. **https://www.loc.gov/item/9750230/**

Opitz, B., Ferdinand, N. K., & Mecklinger, A. (2011). Timing matters: The impact of immediate and delayed feedback on artificial language learning. *Frontiers in Human Neuroscience*, 5(8). **https://doi.org/10.3389/fnhum.2011.00008**

134

REFERENCES

Paul, A. M. (2012, March 18). Your brain on fiction. *The New York Times*, 6.

Peterson, L. (2018, October 17). *The science behind the art of storytelling.* Harvard Business Publishing: Corporate Learning. **https://www.harvardbusiness.org/the-science-behind-the-art-of-storytelling/**

Pink, D. (2013). *Drive: The surprising truth about what motivates us.* Riverhead Books.

Siegesmund, A. (2016). Increasing student metacognition and learning through classroom-based learning communities and self-assessment. *Journal of Microbiology & Biology Education*, 17(2), 204–214. **https://doi.org/10.1128/jmbe.v17i2.954**

Merida, K. *The Undefeated 44: 44 African Americans who shook up the world.* The Undefeated. **https://theundefeated.com/features/the-undefeated-44-most-influential-black-americans-in-history/#introduction/**

Tucker, C. R. (2019). *The on-your-feet guide to blended learning: Station rotation.* Corwin Press.

Vu, V., Warschauer, M., & Yim, S. (2019). Digital storytelling: A district initiative for academic literacy improvement. *Journal of Adolescent & Adult Literacy*, 63(3), 257-267. **https://doi.org/10.1002/jaal.962**

Zak, P. J. (2013, December 13). How stories change the brain. *Greater Good Magazine*. **https://greatergood.berkeley.edu/article/item/how_stories_change_brain**

Index

#

4 C's, 55

15-Second Stories, 112–115

20% Time, 95–96

A

accessibility, 66–68, 69

acrostic poems, 116–118

Adobe Spark, 51, 84, 98

agreement (film), 79–81, 117–118

   assessment of, 71

Aguilar, Niki, 39, 50

Al Jazeera, 25

angles (film), 76–79

animation, 59, 98–99

   assessment of, 72

Animoto, 84, 98, 125

assessment, 69–74

asset collection, 51–52

   specific lessons and, 108, 111, 115, 117–118, 120–121

audio fluency, 81–83

audio literacy, 61, 69, 73, 127

audiovisual planning, 45–47, 59

   specific lessons and, 108, 110, 114

authenticity, 22–23, 99–102

B

Barda, Julie, 28, 88, 131

Beals, Melba Patillo, 109

BioPoems, 43

Black History Month, 23, 110

Bradbury, Ray, 119

brainstorming, 39–41

Bronson, Stephanie, 126, 131

Brown, Valcine, 36, 131

Burns, Ken, 83–84

Butterflies, 28

C

Chauvet Cave, 12

Chavez, Cesar, 109

Christmas Carol, A, 36

Chromebooks, 97–99

Circuit, The, 40, 109

community building, 101–102

Corippo, Jon, 82

cortisol, 16

COVID-19 pandemic, 125–126

Creative Commons, 81

Creative Communicator (ISTE Standards), 56, 107, 110, 113, 116, 119

critical cop-outs, 49

critical friends, 49

Cruz, Mario, 65, 131

D

Damasio, Antonio, 17

Dear Mr. President, 29–31

Depth of Knowledge (DOK), 63

Descartes, René, 17

Descartes' Error, 17

Diaz Cuevas, Susan, 95, 131

DiBari, Sherry, 37, 67, 131

DiCamillo, Kate, 128

Dickens, Charles, 36

DIGICOM Learning, 8–9, 18, 53, 64, 84, 131

Digital Citizen (ISTE Standards), 57, 107, 110, 116, 119

digital storytelling, 14

    barriers to, 89–102

    educational benefit of, 16–19, 56–63

    as an emotional outlet, 25–28

    equalizing power of, 22–25

    ISTE Standards and, 56–57

    Storytelling Saves the World podcast, 30

disabilities, students with, 66–68

dopamine, 16

Drive, 17

E

Eastwood, Clint, 15

editing, 52, 86–87

    assessment of, 72

    specific lessons and, 108, 111–112, 115, 118, 121

Edpuzzle, 127

EduProtocol Field Guide, The, 82

effects and transitions, 87, 121

    assessment of, 72

emotion, 14–17, 41–43, 85–87

    storytelling as an outlet for, 25–28

Empowered Student (ISTE Standards), 107, 116, 119

English Language Development (ELD), 93–95

English language learners, 6, 66–67, 93–95

Epic of Gilgamesh, 12

F

Fahrenheit 451, 119

Family, 24–25

feedback, 48–51, 54, 69–74, 85–88

    online instruction and, 126, 129–130

    specific lessons and, 107–108, 110–111, 114, 117, 120

Ferrés, Joan, 17, 19

Ferris Bueller's Day Off, 82

film angles, 76–79

film grammar, 75–76

Finneran, Max, 131

FlipGrid, 124

Flores, Ricardo, 61, 68, 131

Frakes, Shane, 124, 131

Frayer models, 39–40

Fulton, Larry, 131

G

Gamboa, Virginia, 44, 131

Genius Hour, 95

Gitto, Maria, 131

Global Collaborator (ISTE Standards), 57

Glows and Grows, 53, 130

Golden Share (principle), 100–101

Google Classroom, 126, 129–130

Google Docs, 126

Google Drive, 129

Google Images, 80–81

Google Meet, 125, 129

Grafton, Lee, 7–8, 62, 94, 131

griots, 13

Guttler, Frank, 92, 131

H

haiku, 127–128

Harvey Milk Diversity Breakfast
(Palm Springs), 28

Hebern, Marlena, 82

Horse in Motion, The, 13

Hurley, Rushton, 53

I

"I Am" poems, 43, 64, 66–68, 106–109

immigrants and immigration, 29–32

iMovie, 5–6, 65, 84, 96–98

"In My Time" Project, 109–112

Innovative Designer (ISTE Standards), 57

interdisciplinary collaboration, 62–63

iPads, 65, 96–98

ISTE Standards for Students, 56–57
specific lessons and, 107, 110, 113, 116, 119

J

Jimenez, Francisco, 40, 109

Journal of the American Academy of Child and
Adolescent Psychiatry, 123

K

Kahoot! 114

Ken Burns Effect, 83–84

Khan Academy, 42

Knowledge Constructor (ISTE Standards), 57,
107, 110, 113, 116, 119

L

Library of Congress, 94–95, 111

Limits, 30–31

Lost Ships, 4

LQBTQ+ students, 28

Lyon, George Ella, 44

M

Masanet, Maria-Jose, 17, 19

McKee, Norman, 13, 29, 131

Meadows, Daniel, 14

mise en place, 75

Mote (voice comments extension), 120

moviemaking process, 37–54

music, 22–23, 46, 82–83, 86–87, 111–112
assessment of, 71

N

Next Generation Science Standards
(NGSS), 58

O

One Day at a Time, 27

O'Neil, Jamie, 100, 131

online instruction, 123–126, 127–130

oxytocin, 16

P

Pack, Brandon, 69, 131

Paleolithic era, 12

Palm Springs, California, 18–19, 31

Palm Springs International Film Festival, 4

Pexels, 51

Pink, Daniel, 17

pitch groups, 48–51, 114

Pixabay, 51

Pixar in a Box, 42

Plato, 15

Policy Analysis for California Education, 6

Powtoon, 59, 98

preproduction, 45, 93

   See also audiovisual planning; scripting

public service announcements (PSAs), 7–8, 31, 60–61

publishing, 53–54

   specific lessons and, 108–109, 112, 116, 118, 121

Q

Quarantine Voices project, 125–126, 132

Quizizz, 114

R

reflection, 74, 96, 126

Remembering Gio, 26–27

representation, 22–25

resilience, 125

resources for lessons, 122

revision, 38, 52, 93

Ruiz, Raul, 30

S

Salmi, Greta, 131

Salton Sea, 3

Sauer, Brad, 131

SCALE, 49–50, 84–88, 131

   online instruction and, 127, 129

screen grammar, 75–76

scripting, 41–44, 59

   specific lessons and, 107, 110, 114, 117, 120

self-efficacy, 18–19

SoundBible, 51

station rotation, 73–74, 92–93, 97

STEM, 36–37, 58–59, 109, 113

story spines, 42–43, 66, 119–122

storyboards, 45–46

Storytelling Saves the World, 30–31

T

technology, 18–19, 96–99

templates

   abbreviated "I Am" poem template, 67

   accessibility and, 66

   "OurFlix" template, 130

   specific lesson templates, 122

   storyboard templates, 45–46

   storytelling templates, 42–44

Terlaje, Georgia, 30–31, 53, 58, 131

three-act structure, 41–42

Tiger Rising, The, 128

TikTok, 124, 125

time, finding, 90–95

Toontastic, 59, 98

INDEX

transitions and effects, 87, 121
    assessment of, 72
Tucker, Catlin, 93
two-column notes, 46–47
Tyson, Neil deGrasse, 109

U

Undefeated 44, The, 24, 110
undocumented immigrants, 29–30
University of California Riverside, 18–19

V

Videvo, 51
visual literacy, 61, 69, 73, 127
Vogel, David, 7–9, 18, 42, 92, 131
voiceovers, 81–83, 99, 118
    assessment of, 71
Vu, Viet, 19

W

Warriors Don't Cry, 109
Warschauer, Mark, 19
Webb, Norman, 63
WeVideo, 51–52, 84, 98, 124, 125
"Where I'm From," 44
Without Him, 27
writing
    students who struggle with, 66
    See also Scripting

Y

Yada, Lynn, 30–31, 47, 131
Yim, Soobin, 19
YouTube, 32, 53, 84, 125

Z

Zoom (software), 129

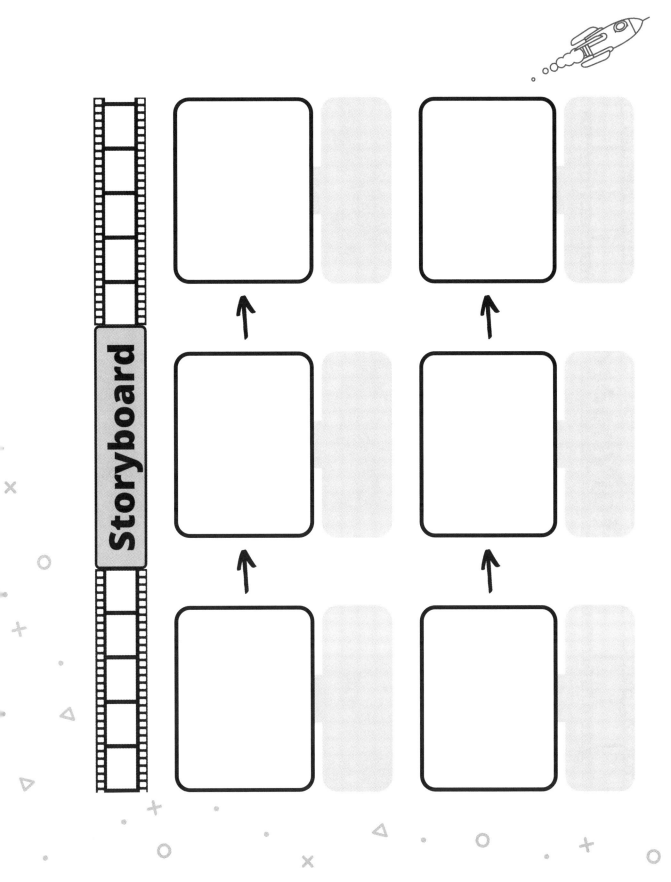

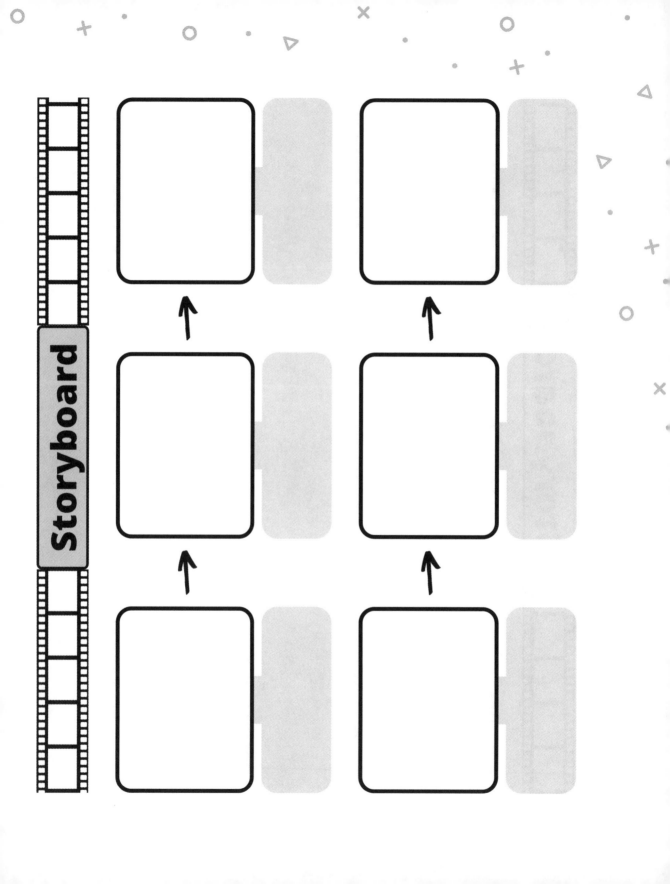

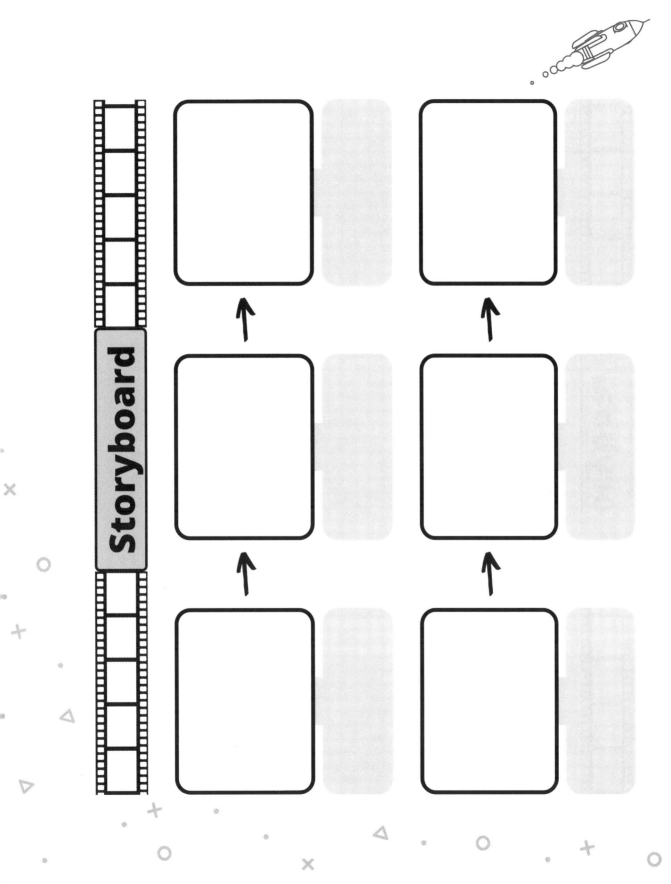

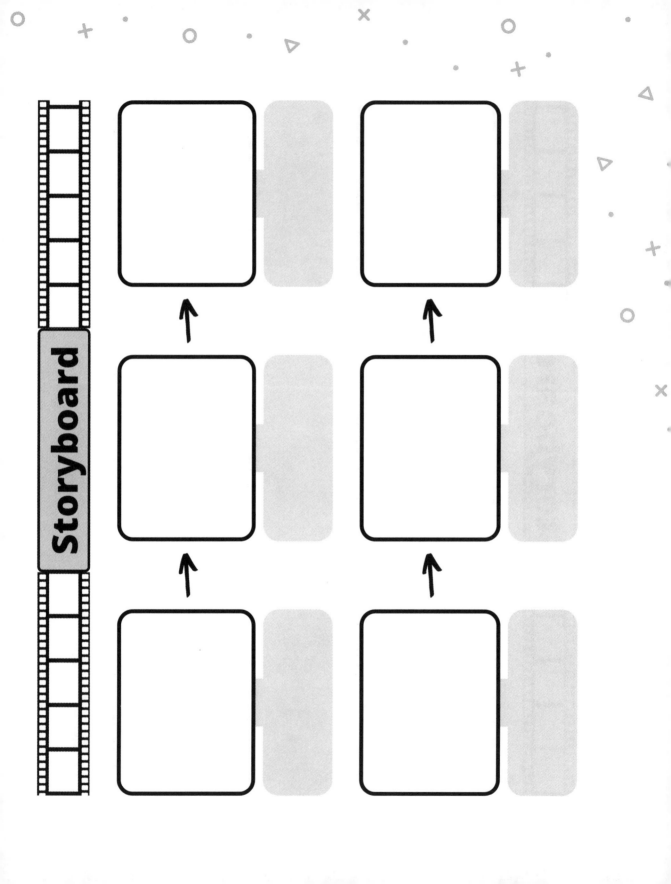

Storyboard

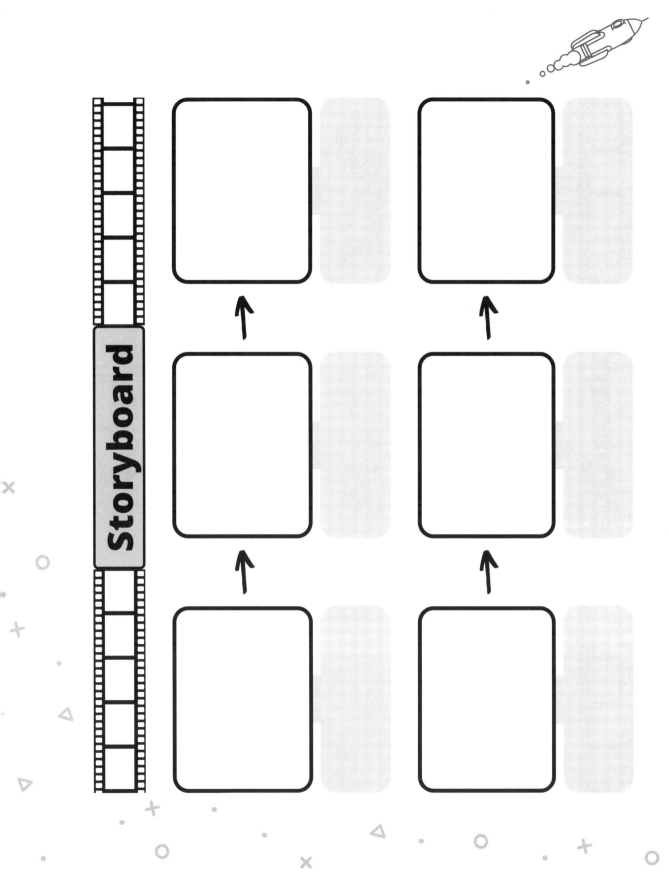

Storyboard

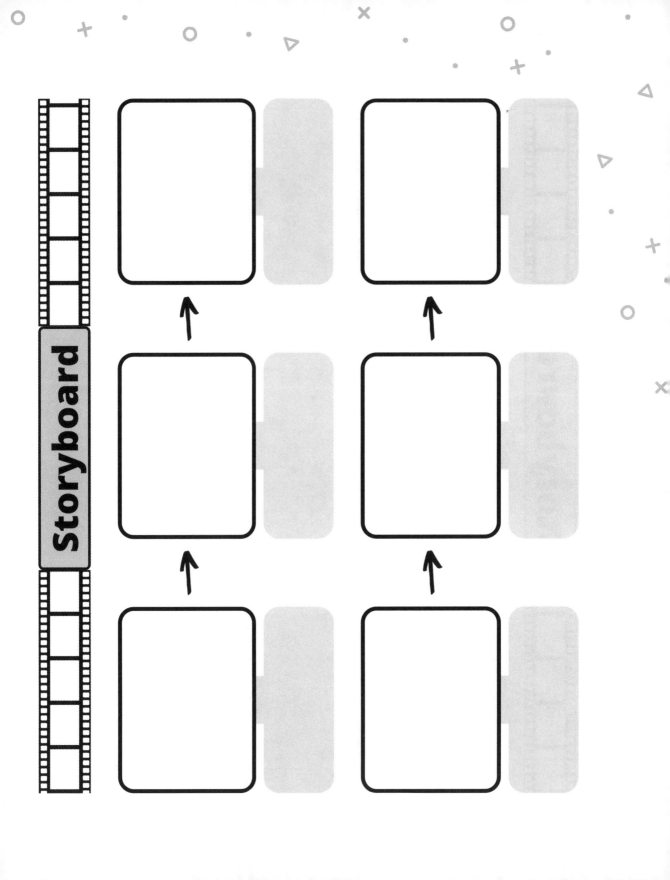

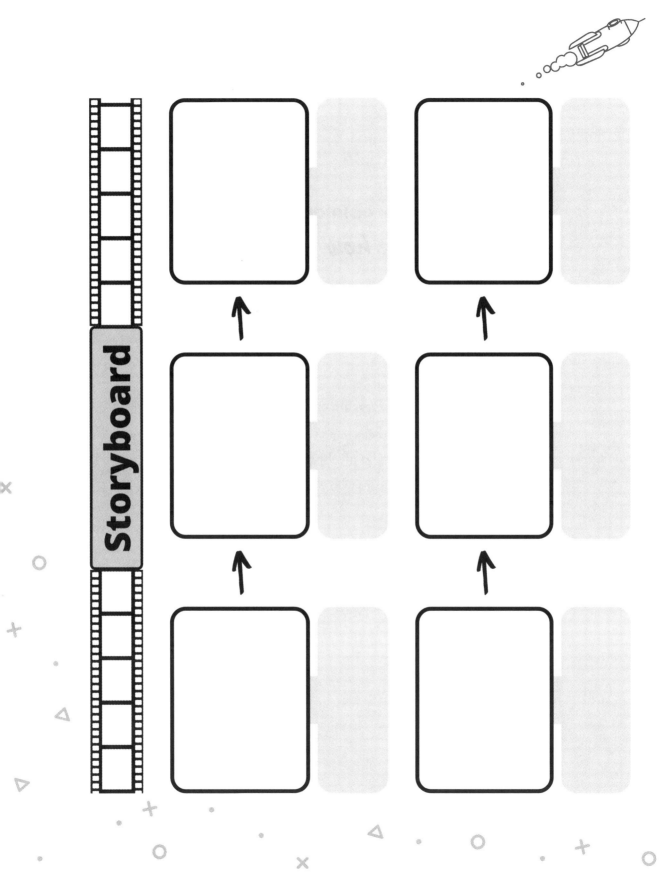

Storyboard

Your opinion matters:
Tell us how we're doing!

Your feedback helps ISTE create the best possible resources for teaching and learning in the digital age. Share your thoughts with the community or tell us how we're doing!

You can:

✦ Write a review at **amazon.com** or **barnesandnoble.com**.

✦ Mention this book on social media and follow ISTE on Twitter @iste, Facebook @ISTEconnects or Instagram @isteconnects.

✦ Email us at books@iste.org with your questions or comments.